How I Saved My Own Life

How I Saved My Own Life

and You Can Too!

ANN HAMILTON WALLACE

Sonrise Publishing

(LOGO) Sonrise Publishing

Copyright © 2016 Ann Hamilton Wallace
All rights reserved.

ISBN-13: 9780984566303
ISBN-10: 0984566309
Library of Congress Control Number: 2016904610
Sonrise Publishing, Marina Del Rey, CA

Dedication

I dedicate this book to my Creator. He/She has given me more time to be with my family in a meaningful way and the artistic inspiration and energy to complete this book.

Contents

Acknowledgments

My family, for giving me a good reason to live and be here for them!

To my true friends, the ones who motivate and inspire me, are there when things sometimes get tough, you know who you are. Grazie mili

Dr. Armando Giuliano, Dr. Jay Orringer, Dr. Parvis Gamigami, Dr. Robert Katz and Dr. James Waisman for the best care anyone could hope for.

A special thank you to Deborah Ansley Allen for deciphering my handwritten notes and entering them into the computer.

My husband, Larry Wallace and son, Jon Wallace for nurturing me back to health. I love both of you so much.

Rosa Clark for introducing me to two great books that I used for the chapters on food and herbs.

Dr. Jay Orringer, a special thank you for the time you spent on the manuscript correcting medical terminology and encouraging me along the way.

Vicki Torres, for editing.

Paige Craig for the beautiful cover photo.

Nancy Younan Tamer for another great book cover design

To the authors, publishing houses, and Los Angeles Times for graciously permitting use of copyright material in this book, thank you, thank you, thank you!

Introduction

With no family history of breast cancer and because I followed the accepted norms of a healthy life, when I was diagnosed with the condition I was astonished to find myself suddenly having to battle for my health and perhaps even my life.

The diagnosis was the beginning of a journey of research and discovery. Therefore, you will find in this book a compilation of information I gathered while having a mastectomy and the resulting determination to help others avoid the pitfalls of not knowing.

Reading and note taking were my constant occupations while gathering research to write. Having tons of gratitude and praying my experience in someway might help others, propelled me through each surgery countless post- operation appointments and meetings with my oncologist.

Afterwards, I was grateful for the gift of time that I had to be able to gather information and learn so much new information. I was especially grateful during those times I would get on a soapbox and caution friends about the dangers of drinking, antibiotic use, etc. and no one knew a thing about it!

We might all assume in this age of computers, that everyone knows the information out there. But sometimes it's tricky to retrieve what you want and then again one must have time on their hands to do it.

Also, some of us are under the misconception that family history is everything when it comes to breast cancer. Contributing factors won't affect us if we don't have the BRCA gene. This false thinking is serious business and almost cost me my life.

In keeping with this idea that most woman are very busy, I gathered the information in this book and wrote my opinions in non-repetitive, lay terms. The data is admittedly non-exhaustive but it is designed to impart the most important information. Perhaps further exploration of your own would be helpful to you.

Please consider that this is my story and my research. The information is to get you thinking about how to protect yourself from breast cancer. I want you to have your own healthy story and I wish all of you happy endings.

SECTION 1

MY STORY

One

An Unexpected Diagnosis

How does one start a book as life changing or challenging as this one? By starting at the beginning. In the beginning of my odyssey I thought I was immune to breast cancer. After all, none of my aunts and grandmothers or mother had even had a breast biopsy. Therefore, I enjoyed a certain peace of mind about growing older. I was living a life of thoughtful contemplation. I started eating organic foods and moved to the beach, Marina del Rey, surrounded by Los Angeles but where the air was cleaner. Surely, not smoking, getting in some walking and quiet moments would do the trick.

I felt fairly youthful and sailed through menopause with the help of Dr. Uzzi Reiss and hormone replacement therapy (HRT). Dr. Reiss prescribed many supplements and I took Vitamin B12 shots regularly. With a sense of false bravado, I neglected many screenings, which did not get done in a timely manner, while I took care of my autistic son. This child had been long-awaited and yearned for; he is my only son. I found a cause to fight for and fighting is what I did. As an advocate for Jon, I debated endlessly with doctors and the school district about his rights and what "was in the best interest of the child."

For this reason, a regular colonoscopy that was advised to do at age 50 got put off until age 58! My mammograms were done every three to five years. Most women know that after age 50, the medical establishment recommends a mammogram every year.

I finally scheduled a colonoscopy after a dear friend was suddenly diagnosed with colon cancer. We were the same age and my courage was a little shaken. I did not know at the time the enormity of the challenge ahead.

The day of the colonoscopy I had the usual jitters about anesthesia and what the doctor might find. Putting on a brave face, I decided to do a hemorrhoidectomy at the same time. While he was up there we agreed to snip a few appendages. When I awoke the doctor explained he found a large polyp. The polyp was large enough to recommend tests every three years instead of five! I was so thankful I dodged the bullet and had a chance to live.

With renewed energy, I began a running program on the beach. After all, this was a chance to be new and improved, like fine wine. The sand was soft and the ocean breeze encouraged every effort.

It was true what the experts said about exercise, I could feel a sense of calm and a surge of energy with every step. I walked home, life was good. But the stairs felt a little different, my left knee would begin to complain as I navigated my way up and down. With additional workouts the knee began hurting more and more and, soon after, I was limping around the Marina. The pain in the knee radiated up to my hip with unending ferocity. I could no longer function. My family doctor recommended physical therapy three times a week. I found a place nearby where the therapists were excellent and the atmosphere was welcoming.

I had runner's knee and had misaligned my facet joint in the lower spine, ouch. For two months I regressed physically on the couch and needed assistance with many things. This was the opposite of what I had planned. By now I thought I would be toned and terrific. I struggled with asking everyone to carry even my purse at times. The day the pain subsided was a day to celebrate. I jumped in the shower, grabbed some shower gel and hurried to get ready for a fabulous day.

In my haste, I pressed a little harder than usual with the shower gel. I felt something alarming. Is this what a breast lump feels like? It was like a thickening under the left nipple. When I pressed down it was a little sore. I had heard cancer doesn't hurt, that's why so many women don't know they have it.

At that time, I was feeling a little vulnerable and not so self-assured; therefore, as I leapt out of the shower the phone was in my other hand. I called Dr. Parvis Gamagami's office at the Breast Center in Van Nuys. A friend of mine explained the situation to the staff. I was put on hold for a very long time which didn't sit well with either of us. When a breast lump is inconveniently discovered, at an inappropriate moment nothing else matters and one expects the world to acknowledge your urgency. The soonest appointment available was one week later. Putting the matter out of my mind seemed a healthy thing to do. I busied myself with all the demands of a modern woman.

A week later I arrived with my friend at the Breast Center. She tried everything to distract me from the unpleasant task at hand.

We walked the waiting room floor, we talked and read magazines and made phone calls. The phone calls didn't make us popular with the other patients but we hardly noticed; our world had become self-centered at that moment. The calling of my name was an approach-avoidance situation. I was glad not to have to wait any longer but did not really want to have invasive procedures.

My doctor was very well regarded in the medical community and had been featured on the television news program. "20/20." Dr. Gamagami was the best at detecting any cancerous lesion that might exist in a mammogram. Therefore, one could be assured – if Dr. Gamagami told them not to worry, you didn't have to worry.

Dr. Gamagami and I started a polite conversation about the last few days. I reiterated the details and soon was led to the squeeze machine. I call the mammography machine the squeeze machine because in Dr. William Campbell Douglass, Jr.'s essay entitled "Mammography Madness" he writes about the dangers of the so-called proper technique.

"Techniques used are designed for maximum detection of cancerous tissue without regard to the possible disastrous consequences. One survey found that the mammographers used as much compression as the patient could tolerate and had no idea how much compression they were actually using. As the guidelines state, for proper mammography, adequacy of compression device is crucial to good quality mammography. In other words, squeeze the hell out of the breast for clear pictures and just forget about the Hippocratic admonition to do the patient no harm. The recommended force to be used in order to compress the breast tissue enough for a proper mammogram is 300 newtons. That's the equivalent of stacking 50 one pound bags of sugar on the breast."

After the procedure I met with the doctor. He entered the room with a smile on his face, that is always a good sign after a mammogram.

"It seems, Mrs. Wallace, your test is perfect," he beamed.

"I guess that's good, Doctor, but I feel a lump under the skin of my left breast!"

I wasn't going anywhere until we determined what the lump was. My mind now began to reassure me it was all those cups of coffee that probably formed fibrocystic changes in the breast. Furthermore, mammograms show cancer if you have it, don't they???

As we walked into an exam room with the ultrasound equipment I felt a little less concerned.

Dr. Gamagami performed a manual exam and confirmed my findings. He felt a lump in my left breast. This led to, as many women have experienced, an ultrasound examination. An ultrasound is painless and shows many things a mammogram misses.

The doctor found the mass and performed a needle biopsy. In the hands of a doctor like Dr. Gamagami the needle biopsy is more uncomfortable mentally than it is physically.

I got dressed and went on a scheduled visit to see my daughter in Seattle. The time spent with my family was the best medicine. Soon after, I settled into the thought that all was well.

When I came home, messages were waiting on a full answering machine. This is common when most people return from an escape! Going through all of them was not unpleasant, hearing from friends saying they missed me. One greeting from Dr. Gamagami was distressing, "Mrs. Wallace we found irregular cells from the needle biopsy. Therefore, we will have to do core biopsy as soon as possible back at the office."

Irregular cells, what does that mean? Without hesitation, I made an appointment. I reached out to my new neighbor who was rapidly becoming a best friend.

The anticipation of the procedure was a little unnerving. This time instead of a needle, a probe would be thrust into the breast area. I thought if I could only be brave and not squirm around just one more time.

Flat on my back and not for any pleasurable reason, I grimaced as the local anesthetic was injected into several areas of my breast.

It was time for the moment of truth. Within a few seconds a piece of my genetics would be plucked and placed on a slide for expert examination. As fast as greased lightning the biopsy was safely on the slide which was placed on a silver tray.

Taking time to exhale was good. This ensured that I would not faint and expire from a cracked skull. After all, the cells were "irregular" and maybe this biopsy would clear the way for some peace of mind.

Five days later, I returned to the Breast Center to discuss the tests results. When the doctor entered the examination room, I scanned his face for reassurance. Dr. Gamagami smiled and said hello to me and my friend, Ansley, who was holding my hand ever so tightly.

"Mrs. Wallace, your test results were not satisfactory," he said.

I always wondered how a doctor told a patient they had cancer, especially a doctor with such class as this one.

"Okay, what's next?" I said.

I encourage you to call Dr. Armando Guliano at St. John's Hospital for a consultation.

My friend Ansley had Dr. Guliano's number and was dialing his office before I was finished with Dr. Gamagami. I grilled the doctor for 10 more minutes about what all this meant.

"This means you must have surgery to remove the cancer as soon as possible," Dr. Gamagami said, adding, "I must tell you, Mrs. Wallace, you're the only patient I have to tell today that has a good prognosis. Three other women will get news that is much more serious than yours.

I felt a sudden sadness come over me. Knowing other women had to struggle more or might not make it, how devastating!!!! This made me want to cry and at the same time find a way to prevent others from experiencing the same heartbreak.

Ansley and I left the Breast Center and went straight to our local hangout. We ordered our martinis and the bartender asked what we were celebrating. I answered that I have the less aggressive type of cancer and my prognosis is good!

Now was the time to find the reason in all of this, and turn my suffering into a way to help others. While I'm on the subject of martinis, limit, limit, limit them!!! Once spirits were for annual celebratory events and traditional rituals; now they are consumed in alarming quantities. Guilty of my own consumption, I was over the legal limit for breast cancer risk! After all, I did not get drunk or even have a second drink but I did have two or more alcoholic beverages in a day. I thought a glass of wine with lunch and a beer at the football game was reasonable.

My cancer was a learning process and an eye-opening experience. Studying with a specific purpose in mind does motivate one to work hard. The information available about alcohol consumption and breast cancer was coming to a head. The day I was scheduled to see Dr. Guiliano the TV in the waiting room was blaring the grim findings about alcohol consumption and the added risk of breast cancer. I thought of all my friends and family and began to compile information. Information about how many variables exist that influence the risk of getting the dreaded diagnosis.

Therefore, you will find in this book a compilation of information I gathered while having a mastectomy and the resulting determination to help others avoid the pitfalls of not knowing

THE VALUE OF GETTING A SECOND OPINION

How many of us know that getting a second opinion is absolutely necessary when facing a serious illness? We know, but often are exhausted by our illness and do not want to offend our doctors, that sometimes have become our friends and who our lives may depend on. Consider the fact that if our doctors really are friends they will encourage and want us to get that second opinion. The following article is an example in point.

Los Angeles Times, California, Sunday, September 7, 2008
Article by Steve Lopez, Points West.

CANCER, ASK PLENTY OF QUESTIONS

When I first wrote about my sister's health problems earlier this year, a Cedars-Sinai doctor I know called to ask if he could help in any way. Actually, I said, "I'd appreciate a referral to a good oncologist."

What's happened since then is a cautionary tale for anyone who gets sick.

My sister, Debbie, 57, was diagnosed with ovarian cancer about 2 ½ years ago. She lives in Northern California, where we both were raised, and she got excellent care from her managed-care provider. I'm withholding the name of the provider because when I spoke with doctors there, it was as a concerned brother rather than as a journalist.

A large tumor was surgically removed from my sister's abdomen. Then she underwent grueling bouts of chemotherapy and radiation, and began her recovery. Just when she was feeling herself again, she got more terrible news. In June, an MRI revealed a brain tumor the size of a golf ball.

The doctors said it was possible that the tumor was benign, unconnected to her previous cancer. Surgical removal showed otherwise. My sister's growth was a carcinoma. Her ovarian cancer had metastasized.

When Debbie got well enough to visit her oncologist, he strongly recommended she undergo whole-brain radiation over other treatments, so she resigned herself to the procedure. Meanwhile, I began doing a little research. The median survival rate for someone who has surgery followed by whole-brain radiation, according to one often-quoted study, is 23 months. I also learned that there can be significant side effects from whole-brain radiation, including memory, hearing and vision loss. I found the news so grim, I withheld it from my sister until she'd regained her strength. She had said, by the way, that her doctor had led her to believe that side effects from whole-brain radiation are often minimal and don't show up for years.

In the meantime, I called the doctor recommended by my friend at Cedars. When she heard the details of my sister's case, the doctor, one of the nation's leading specialists in women's cancers, strongly recommended that we get a second opinion—because from what I was describing, whole-brain radiation might not be necessary.

She also disagreed on another point, saying side effects from the procedure were not uncommon, often immediate and potentially severe. In similar cases, she recommended gamma knife radiation for her patients, a more localized treatment that doesn't kill anywhere near as many healthy cells. If the cancer returned, as it often does, that would be the time for whole-brain radiation, she said.

I called my sister with the news and she decided to hold off on a decision. Meanwhile, I spoke to two more prominent oncologists who backed the doctor from Cedars-Sinai, one of them emphatically.

He said the approach recommended to my sister was old-school medicine.

My sister's oncologist disagreed. If she wanted the gamma knife, he told me, he'd support it. But it would require an out-of-network referral, because his hospital didn't have the equipment.

"If she were my sister, I'd recommend whole-brain radiation," he said, insisting that the procedure was the best way to ward off any recurrence for the longest period of time.

He's a doctor, I'm not.

Should I stay out of it?

Not a chance.

I called the experts I'd spoken to earlier with more specific information about the cell structure of my sister's surgically removed tumor. Based on what I was telling them, they stuck with the gamma knife recommendation, and my sister's own research had led to the same conclusion.

So what was going on? Was the managed-care doctor's recommendation based on good medicine and familiar protocol, or on the company's aversion to out-of-network expenses?

I got the names of specialists at the University of California San Francisco Medical Center, and my sister's oncologist agreed to send her there for a second opinion. The referral process was maddening, and my sister found battling the bureaucracy almost as tough as trying to recover from brain surgery.

In the end, a team of UCSF doctors barely considered the whole-brain radiation.

Their recommendation?

Gamma knife surgery.

I began wondering about all the people who might have undergone whole-brain radiation, and had their quality of life diminished, because they were not told enough about other options. And how many thousands of times does that happen with other illnesses?

My sister had the advantage of a hell-raising brother who's accustomed to rattling cages and demanding answers. And I was lucky enough to know a doctor who gave me an entrée. But Jamie Court of Consumer Watchdog advises all patients to ask tough questions of their doctors.

"If the best treatment isn't in the HMO network," he said, "the patient may never hear about it. Even if it's the most likely way to save their life."

To learn more about your right to a second medical opinion, Court suggested visiting www.calpatientguide.org.

Mike Bidart, a Claremont lawyer, has represented several clients who were denied gamma knife treatment. He said he's won out-of-court settlements in each case, but only after tough fights.

There's no doubt that cost is a consideration in medicine, said Art Caplan, a medical ethicist at the University of Pennsylvania. And it should be, of course. We can't all expect to get referrals for *every treatment available, while at the same time screaming about high cost of healthcare. But Caplan added that it's a doctor's duty to lay out all the known options for a patient with a deadly disease.*

My sister underwent gamma knife surgery three weeks ago at UCSF and is doing well, volunteering in her spare time to raise money for cancer research. Her managed-care provider has said it will pick up at least part of the bill this time, but perhaps not if she needs surgery again.

She knows, as we all do, that the cancer may return. But she's strong and willing to keep fighting, whether the foe is cancer, an HMO or both. Steve.lopez@latimes.com

Two

SURREAL SURGERY

I recently saw Christina Applegate on television and knew what she had gone through. God bless you, Christina and your courageous decision to remove both breasts!

From the moment you meet with your surgeon, everything is surreal. Your surgeon gives you lots of options, lumpectomy with radiation, mastectomy with or without chemotherapy, remove one breast, remove two breasts, remove breast with reconstruction, with implants, behind the muscle wall or in front of it, with nipple reconstruction, or without, etc.

I spent eight hours talking to doctors on several days preceding my surgery.

At this time your support system is very important. Even those women who pride themselves on being caretakers must reach out for help. The amount of information is overwhelming and often you are in a state of shock.

You can expect to have any modesty put aside. Examinations and pictures are taken at every conceivable angle and not in candlelight. I began to feel a slight disconnect with my body. Thinking back, I saw this as the gift. I always knew I am not my body but the ego pulls us back into illusions.

Dr. Guiliano's reputation precedes him: master surgeon, saver of lives, purveyor of hope.

I was determined to change the mood of our first visit from sterile to soiree. Dr. G would be the host and I would be the guest of honor. To start things off, I told him of my Italian heritage. He replied, I don't treat my Italian patients any differently than all my other patients. Oops, my attempt at ice breaking was just met with the big chill.

It became clear to me now that the doctor did not condone any attempt at denial. Our meeting was serious business and the sooner I behaved accordingly the happier the doctor would be.

After serious consideration I opted for a mastectomy. My breasts were not large and a lumpectomy with clear margins would be deforming anyway. I did not think radiation would be a good idea at my age and also could make my fibromyalgia worse. The decision being made was some sort of relief in itself. But the surgery was not a walk in the park.

Even in Dr. G's hands, the result was disfiguring and the pain unusually rough. I kept taking myself off the pain meds for fear of becoming addicted only to find I needed to go back on them.

This is the time when family and friends as well as good doctors can save your life, not only physically but emotionally as well.

With the surgery behind me, it was time for the reconstruction phase of my treatment. In surgery at the time of my mastectomy and assisting, Dr. G was an extraordinary man, superb doctor and soon to become a family friend.

Enter Dr. Jay Orringer. Dr. Orringer "resides" in a penthouse in Beverly Hills where he sees patients nonstop sometimes working 18-hour days. He is considered the top doctor in his field of reconstructive plastic surgery of the breast.

The ladies in the front office are always warm and reassuring making a visit to Dr. Orringer's a happy occasion. The blue gowns in the examining room have been specially designed by Ana Marie, Padi, and Dr. Orringer to flatter your appearance and make your visit more pleasant. Padi makes you feel like a long-lost friend and that is a wonderful thing.

At the time of my mastectomy, Dr. Orringer inserted an expander. The expander stretches the skin in preparation for an implant. I was told the expander is not the most comfortable part of this reconstruction process. The expander feels a little icky because of the metal port that stays in place for three months. Nevertheless, Dr. Orringer has a terrific way of making a person feel good. He is generous with his time, remembers small details about your family and even likes your children. My son, Jon, was happily included in all of the prep sessions for my surgery and Dr. Orringer spent special time with him making him feel involved in my care.

I remember asking Dr. Orringer if the mastectomy and the implants could be done at the same time. He reassured me that was not in my best interest. Dr. Orringer is a perfectionist (whenever possible) and always tries to make women feel good about themselves after breast cancer surgery. The meticulous details of sizing the breasts, expanding the skin, revising scars and grafting the nipple are all second nature to Dr. Orringer. That is why some of the best breasts in town are created by his genius.

After three months had passed I was ready to lose the expander and get my small breast implants. Even though the implants are small they are placed behind the pectoral muscles, which makes recovery quite painful. I remember getting sick to my stomach often from the combination of pain meds plus antibiotics. Dr. Orriginer is so careful with every detail that it is why antibiotics are necessary for aftercare. An implant is a foreign body and one wants to be sure no infection gets started after surgery.

As I was healing I noted that thanks to Dr. Orringer, both breasts looked very similar. The only drawback was that they didn't feel the same.

The unaffected breast still felt very natural and had sensitivity in the nipple. The left breast felt like a grapefruit was inserted into the breast and it had very little sensitivity with no existing nipple. As I pondered the situation I was assuring myself that Dr. Orringer's work would be impeccable and the absence of the cancer was a blessing. As I was reassuring myself, a little more drama erupted in my life; Dr. Reiss called and explained that my pelvic ultrasound from the previous year was not looking good. I said, "What?"

How come no one let me know about this? It became apparent that too many cooks in the kitchen spoil the broth. Because I had two gynecologists, one for my usual exams and one for hormone replacement, each doctor thought that the other one had alerted me. Putting blame aside I called a doctor in Beverly Hills that Dr. Reiss recommended. Dr. Robert Katz was very kind; he took me into his care quickly to make sure no more time was lost. Here it was, only three and one-half weeks after my last surgery and I was under the knife again. This time it was to remove a large polyp and do a D&C (dilation and curettage). The polyp and other specimens were sent to the lab. Now, I had to wait one agonizing week to find out if I still had cancer. If so, I would have to have a hysterectomy and maybe even chemotherapy. Dr. Katz was concerned about the possibility that the uterine cancer may have preceded the breast cancer. The possibility of a metastasis was horrifying. I decided to conjure up all my faith in God's goodness and planned for the best.

One thing I learned from this experience is to get a copy of all your tests. At one time the labs automatically sent copies to the doctors and the patients. Now it is your responsibility to call your doctor and ask for a personal copy for your records. If I had done this I would have seen the problem a year earlier. Sometimes one year can make the difference between life and death. And don't always believe no news is good news; at times it means someone has dropped the ball.

Just as I had been an advocate for my son, Jon, I would have to advocate for myself. As I waited with family and friends for the news, everyone was hoping for the best. After all, God doesn't give us more than we can handle, does She? Finally, Dr. Katz called with the good news; all the specimens were benign!

I thanked Dr. Katz for his good care and began my inventory of blessings. I had been so blessed from the beginning to have my colon polyp be negative; I had been blessed to find my breast cancer when it was so small.

Dr. Orringer actually said, "Who found this lump when it was so small?"

I said, I did.

He replied, "You saved your own life."

And finally to get the news I had been waiting for from my pelvic surgery, all specimens were benign.

The fantastic results coupled with generous support from my family and friends made me feel over the moon!

I basked in the feeling that God was my constant companion, all the time knowing that those who are given much, are asked much of.

I now dreaded meeting with my oncologist, the word that makes most people shutter. My past experience with oncology was not a good one. My father had lung cancer 25 years ago. As he lay on his deathbed gasping for air, his oncologist entered the room and suggested shooting gold into his veins, a very painful process. I remember asking him to leave the room immediately and please not to return.

Thank God, oncology has come a long long way since then. It is still prudent to select your oncologist wisely. Dr. Giuliano suggested an oncologist in Santa Monica where I live. After discussing the doctor's ultraconservative nature and talking with a friend who was treated by this doctor, I chose Dr. James Waisman, M.D., instead. It seems my friend felt she was treated so aggressively that sometimes she thought she wasn't going to make it through the process. I am happy to report my friend is doing well and her beautiful spirit has not been dampened.

I choose Dr. Waisman for several reasons. First, Dr. Orringer who was now a part of the family recommended him.

Secondly, Dr. Waisman was known to think outside the box. By outside the box I mean he doesn't suggest chemo, etc. unless the benefits greatly outweigh the risks. For someone like me who is not so young and has fibromyalgia a round of chemotherapy could be devastating to my body and probably my family as well. Other therapies such as tamoxifen can greatly alter one's quality of life. Dr. Waisman said he thought tamoxifen would not be a bad treatment for me since my cancer was estrogen and progesterone sensitive. After we discussed the possibility of that treatment I explained my concerns.

"It just comes down to quality of life, doesn't it?" Dr. Waisman asked, and I replied, yes. In other words you don't put someone on tamoxifen for five years, which can make you feel like hell, to reduce your risk on recurrence by 9%.

Before I left the office, Dr. Waisman meticulously presented the details of my condition to my husband and me in a one-hour session. In this session he used a computer to calculate the benefits of additional therapy as opposed to no further treatment. When he put in all the variables such as tumor size, genetic disposition, shape of the cells, my age and aggressiveness of the cancer, he concluded no further treatment was necessary. At that moment, I felt like I had won the lottery, and in some respects I guess I had.

Joy rushed over me and I vowed not to sweat the small stuff.

Driving home with my husband, I felt a great sense of satisfaction. I was satisfied with my life as it was, full of family, friends and more life to live.

I have heard it said, If you are not happy, you are pursuing the wrong goals. My goal now was to be at peace. Obtaining peace would not be difficult if I slowed down, spent more time with my family and began writing my book.

Before I could concentrate on writing I had one more surgery to finish my reconstruction. Dr. Orringer was almost finished putting Humpty Dumpty back together again.

The final step in my process was a left nipple reconstruction. Along the way I gave one nipple up to cancer and now
was the time to collect the one Dr. Orringer promised to give
me back.

Just prior to this last surgery, I returned to see Dr Uzzi Reiss.
Dr. Reiss was the doctor who prescribed hormone replacement
therapy (HRT) for me many years before. HRT was designed
to help me through menopause and keep me feeling the best I
could be.

Since having breast cancer all my doctors wanted me to stop
HRT. I wanted to talk with Dr. Reiss to get his opinion. As I
thought, Dr. Reiss did not waver in his opinion about HRT. He
believed that the research indicating dangers with HRT in the WHI

(Women's Health Initiative) was a flawed study. He explained the hormones used were derived from horse urine and not intended for humans. Because the hormones were not bioidentical, problems exist. After talking with Dr. Reiss and reading some of Suzanne Somers' books, I was determined to make up my own mind. I gave myself some time to decide and I did further research.

The one thing about getting cancer is you feel out of control. Cancer blindsides you, it comes out of nowhere and makes your world tilt off its axis. That is why it is so important to be very involved in your own treatment. Do not say yes to something unless it sits right with you.

Furthermore, Dr. Reiss explained that HRT is not your enemy. Your true enemy is stress. Now that you have had cancer stress can no longer be a factor in your life.

"Let me give you a visual," he said. "Imagine an army of men equipped with machine guns and guarding against any cancer cells in your body. You become stressed, imagine them all sitting around smoking pot. You get the idea?"

So what do you do?

"No stress and eat lots of vegetables."

These were his parting words as he ran down the rabbit hole and left Alice to contemplate her fate.

Soon after my visit with Dr. Reiss, it was time for my fifth surgery. I don't know how many of you have seen the movie, "Groundhog Day." In this movie, Bill Murray is trapped in a drama that keeps happening over and over again. I felt a little like him when all the doctors and nurses at the surgical center knew who I was.

"Mrs. Wallace we are going to put you to sleep now. A little stick and you will be asleep, Mrs. Wallace."

This time, Dr. Orringer appeared and drew details of the surgery on my chest. He did many measurements to be sure the nipple would be placed properly.

Now I was ready for the anesthesiologist to do his magic. Soon I would wake up and return to some form of normalcy. That would be a good thing. Hopefully my family and me could put this chapter behind us and move on to the business of living.

As I awoke hours later, I felt re-energized with the thought that this was the last surgery for a long time. I was grateful I made it through, with little or no side effects. Dr. Orringer was amazed at how well I was healing. I thanked God for my wonderful doctors. I thanked God for the opportunity to cherish life—the opportunity to cherish life even more than I had before!

One week later I was at Dr. Orringer's office for the unveiling. If all went well the nipple would be red, indicating a good blood supply. Luck was again on my side. The graft was a success. The only thing left was a tattoo to complete the look.

As I took time to exhale I made a mental inventory of what I knew. (Don't stress, eat your vegetables, you are not your body,

don't sweat the small stuff, live life to the fullest and when much
is given, much is asked.)

Several months had passed in a flash as I went through my
surgeries and researched contributing factors for breast cancer.
The piles of folders and papers obscured the lamplight designed
to illuminate my desktop. It occurred to me that many women
do not have the luxury of time that I had. I felt determined to
share the information I gathered.

SECTION II
BREAST CANCER RISKS

Three

Internal Risks: Antibiotics, Alcohol, Hormones & Weight

B efore you can start on the right path to health, you need to know the holes and obstacles to avoid. So, I have gathered the information I discovered during my journey and have created this second section comprised of two chapters dealing with risks, internal and external. I hope you find it as eye-opening as I did.

Antibiotic Use

A study by the National Cancer Institute, published in 2004 in the Journal of the American Medical Association (JAMA), provides evidence that use of antibiotics is associated with an increased risk of breast cancer. The authors of this JAMA study found that women who took antibiotics for more than 500 days or had more than 25 prescriptions over a 17-year period had more than twice the risk of breast cancer as women who had not taken any antibiotics. The authors found an increased risk in all classes of antibiotics they studied.

Some researchers speculate that antibiotic use disturbs the body's immune response to inflammation. Destruction of necessary bacteria within the intestines may contribute to the problem. It is possible that people who require more antibiotics for infections might inherently have a weaker immune system and might be more susceptible to the development of cancer. More research must be done, since breast cancer is the second leading cause of cancer deaths among women in the United States. In the meantime, suffice it to say antibiotic use should be limited to bacterial infections.

Long-term uses of low-dose antibiotics for acne have also not been proven safe. Therefore, I believe these regimes should be discontinued. Topical solutions are a safer alternative to dosing the entire body on a daily basis.

At this time, no clear-cut answers exist to the question about who is at greater risk: women who take low-dose antibiotics for a long period of time or women who take high-dose antibiotics once in a while.

Until all the answers are in, eliminating antibiotic use unless absolutely necessary seems prudent. This is one action women can do to lower the risk of breast cancer.

Alcohol Consumption

Please don't kill the messenger! I know this will not be a popular subject with some of you. I must admit I'm not happy about this research either. But as painful as it might be, we all need to face the facts. And all the facts and research lead to one conclusion:

Alcohol consumption increases the risk of breast cancer. I know the idea of red wine being good for the heart was well received by many. I thought, "How could something that easy and fun be good for you?"

Well, that's the problem with getting a little information and running with it. After my experience with breast cancer, I am determined to research things more thoroughly. Always consider the variables involved before I make any decisions about lifestyle changes. One of my good friends said to me, as I was beginning research on alcohol consumption, "That research cannot have anything to do with wine; Wine is good for you. It must be those women that drink a lot of beer and tequila."

I didn't have the heart to say anything at that time, but further exploration has confirmed my hypothesis that it doesn't matter if the alcohol comes from wine, beer or spirits, the risk for breast cancer goes up in direct proportion to the amount consumed. You may say, "Well, how does this happen?"

All the relevant research points to the conclusion ethanol, or drinking alcohol, in itself is not carcinogenic, but increasing evidence suggests that its metabolic breakdown into acetaldehyde is responsible for the cocarcinogenic affects of alcohol consumption. Acetaldehyde interferes with Vitamin C absorption and other cancer-fighting nutrients we ingest from fruits and vegetables. Acetaldehyde disrupts estrogen metabolism and response, causes cell mutation and can reduce folic acid, also called Vitamin B9, which is essential to numerous body functions. Acetaldehyde significantly increases tumor size and helps microvessel density proliferate within tumors.

"It is generally accepted that the overall risk for breast cancer in women is proportionate to the accumulated lifetime exposure of the breasts to circulating estrogen. For pre- menopausal women, alcohol intake has been linked to higher levels of estrogens, as well as the decreased frequency of prolonged cycles and shorter menstrual periods. These latter two considerations are, in turn, associated with higher estrogen levels and thus increased rates of breast cancer." So read one source I consulted.

Alcohol intake has also been linked to reoccurrence of breast cancer and to the greater development of metastatic breast cancer occurrences, or cancers that spread to other parts of the body from the original tumor site.

Please note, all of you postmenopausal ladies, that alcohol increased the risk for estrogen and progesterone receptor tumors. Just like the one I had. The association between alcohol consumption and breast cancer risk is strongest among postmenopausal women taking HRT concurrently.

Therefore, it is easy to see that chemicalized hormone replacement therapy combined with even moderate amounts of alcohol (two drinks a day) can be a lethal cocktail! Source: Susan M. Gapstur, Ph.D., and Keith W. Singletary, Ph.D., "Alcohol and Breast Cancer," The Journal of the American Medical Association, Vol. 286, No. 17, (Nov. 7, 2001): 2143-2151.

Just when you thought I had abandoned you to a life of lackluster parties and teetotaling, I'm here to tell you about folic acid. As I researched the subject of alcohol's effect on breast cancer risk, a study caught my eye.

Researchers surveyed 17,447 Anglo Australian women, residents of Melbourne, aged 40 to 69 years at recruitment, from 1990 to 1994 and followed up through December 31, 2003. They sought to evaluate the effect of dietary folate intake on the relationship between alcohol consumption and breast cancer.

They found 537 cases of invasive breast cancer among women with a mean age of 54.7. They also found a significant interaction between alcohol and folate intakes. Women who had high alcohol consumption and low intake of folic acid had an increased risk of breast cancer. Women who drank heavily with moderate folate intake appeared to have no increased risk.

Source: Laura Baglietto, Dallas R. English, Dorota M. Gertig, John L. Hopper and Graham G. Giles, "Does Dietary Folate Intake Modify Effect of Alcohol Consumption on Breast Cancer Risk?" British Medical Journal, Vol. 331 (Oct. 8, 2005): 807.

Be careful, there are limitations to this study. One very important factor was the small number of women with high levels of alcohol consumption and folate intake.

Therefore, do not consider these findings a "get out of jail free card." Do consider: An adequate amount of folic acid, approximately 200 mg a day, might protect against the increased risk of breast cancer associated with alcohol consumption. If you must overindulge, please take your folic acid. Always check with your doctor first before taking any supplement suggested in this book, as I am not a medical doctor!

HRT

Hormone replacement therapy…now we are in a very controversial area. Because of all the conflicting research, this section presented the greatest challenge to me. I had to read a great deal of literature online, summarize and introduce my findings in an understandable nonconfounding way. It is my hope, that at the end of this section, you will have enough knowledge to help you make an informed decision about your hormonal needs. You will be able to weigh the risks against the benefits and, with your doctor, choose the best course of action for you. Much of the information I cite comes from Dr. Uzzi Reiss's book, *The Natural Superwoman.*

"When I speak about bioidentical hormones, I am referring to an exact replica of what your body produces. When I mean exact replica, I mean exactly, not almost exactly or most exactly. Anytime you change the smallest thing about a hormone, you change what that hormone does, how that hormone does it, and the consequence of that hormone's actions.

"Small changes to any part of this biochemical dance result in big changes. Anytime science tries to alter or better what the wisdom of women's own bodies produce, catastrophic results ensue."
—Dr. Uzzi Reiss, M.D.

Dr. Reiss gives a great example that demonstrates the safety of bioidentical hormones. He explains that in pregnancy, hormonal changes are extreme: The body's level of two forms of estrogen goes up tenfold, while levels of a third form of estrogen go up a thousandfold. Progesterone goes up a hundredfold.

Even though one's natural hormone levels rise to extreme levels during pregnancy (much more than any HRT product), the risk of breast cancer decreases with each full- term pregnancy.

THE WHI STUDY

Contrast Dr. Reiss' conclusions with the Women's Health Initiative (WHI), whose published findings in 2002 scared the heebie-jeebies out of us. The study sought to test the health consequences of taking replacement estrogen and progesterone. The only problem was that the estrogen and progesterone used in the study are chemicalized versions of our bioidentical hormones.

The WHI concluded that the use of Premarin® and Provera® is associated with breast cancer and cardiovascular disease. The media frenzy began and cautioned women that the use of estrogen might be dangerous. Many women stopped their hormone replacement treatment, and understandably so.

Dr. Reiss warns, "What followed was even more tragic: Millions of women previously on hormone therapy began living with the unpleasant symptoms of estrogen deficiency. The women were also left vulnerable to the many health risks associated with estrogen and progesterone deficiency, including breast cancer and cardiovascular disease."

Dr. Leon Speroff, professor of obstetrics and gynecology at Oregon Health and Science University, and one of the foremost academic authorities on hormone replacement, announced recently, "The negative impact of the Women's Health Initiative is over, we know the study limitations, we know that some of the conclusions promoted in the media were not correct, and we know that the risks that have been promoted by WHI are incredibly small and perhaps not real."

What makes a woman a woman? Estrogen, a group of compounds produced by the body that, together, function as the female sex hormone. If a women is in estrogen deficiency she feels depressed, uninspired, loses her joy for life and often experiences brain fog. Couple this with night sweats, hot flashes and trouble with getting restful sleep and it is evident we are talking about quality of life issues again.

Also E1, E2 and E3, the three major naturally occurring estrogens in women, contribute to the physical functioning of your cardiovascular system, energy levels, inflammation prevention, brain operation, bone support and sexuality. E2, estradiol, is the most potent. E1, estrone, is 85% weaker than E2. E3, estriol, is 99% weaker than E2, but has been shown to provide protection against uterine and breast cancer!

To make the argument for HRT safety, I am citing studies with the most vulnerable group of women: women with breast cancer. These studies are from Dr. Reiss' book, The Natural Superwoman. In one, Dr. Philip J. DiSaia, a gynecological cancer specialist at the University of California, Irvine, treated women with breast cancer using Premarin and Provera. In comparison to nonuser breast cancer patients, those patients using Premarin and Provera enjoyed an 88% survival rate, and nonusers only 63%. The higher survival rates for women with breast cancer on estrogen were also substantiated in a study at M.D. Anderson Cancer Center at the University of Texas.

Additionally, two U.S. studies found similar results, which confirm the safety of estrogen replacement in breast cancer survivors. For example, the second study compared two groups of women with breast cancer, one group taking Premarin and the second group did not. The group assigned to take Premarin included more women with a high-risk, more aggressive form of breast cancer. The study found that the group treated with Premarin had half the deaths and half the metastases of the nontreatment group.

Some doctors still have doubts about prescribing estrogen to women who have had breast cancer. Certain tumors clearly thrive on estrogen, such as tumors of pregnancy; therefore, we acknowledge the need for further research in this area.

PROGESTERONE

Progesterone protects against breast cancer in many ways, including:

1. Converts estradiol to estrone, the weaker form of estrogen, and decreases the rate of buildup.
2. Increases P53, a protein created by a tumor suppressor gene that protects the body from breast cancer.
3. Blocks urokinase plasminogen activator, an enzyme that increases cancer growth.
4. Blocks nuclear factor-kappa beta and Cox-2, proteins that induce inflammation that can contribute to cancer.
5. Protects breast tissue from HER -2/neu oncogene, multiple copies of a gene that can cause tumors to grow more

rapidly and decrease sensitivity to chemotherapy and hormone therapy.

Various studies have shown the benefits of progesterone. A French study of 1,150 women who used bioidentical progesterone cream on their breasts to decrease pain found that those using the cream enjoyed an overall decrease in incidence of breast cancer. Johns Hopkins Medical Center conducted a study on 1,083 women over a period of 30 years. They were divided into two groups, one with low progesterone and another with normal progesterone. They found the low progesterone group had a 5.4-fold higher incidence of perimenopausal breast cancer, a tenfold higher mortality rate from cancer in general, and a threefold higher mortality rate from all causes.

A recent French study of 54,000 women compared two user groups: bioidentical progesterone users and chemical progestin users. Compared to nonusers, the group that used chemical progestin experienced an increase of breast cancer. The group that used bioidentical progesterone had a 10% decrease in breast cancer compared to nonusers.

From everything I read and the studies I saw, a pattern emerged—blanket statements about the safety of hormone replacement therapy are not logical. The testing of bioidentical hormones needs more time, money and consideration by the U.S. Food and Drug Administration (FDA) and many of today's gynecologists. It's amazing to me that so many gynecologists know very little about bioidentical hormones and, therefore, can only prescribe the standard chemicalized versions. What we know about them is not pretty.

For example, Premarin is a form of supplemental estrogen. It is derived from horse urine and is technically called conjugated equine estrogens. The company that makes Premarin claims it's "Natural," meaning it comes from horses. Horses are natural creatures. Horse estrogen is not natural to humans, however.

Premarin contains 10 to 30 or more estrogens, only two are bioidentical to human estrogens. The effect of taking nonhuman estrogens seems clear, based on all the side effects and the statistical findings in WHI.

After my surgery, I had to make a very important decision. I had just had breast cancer in my left breast, but I opted to preserve my right breast. Therefore, I needed to be extra careful with my "lifestyle" decisions in the future. There I go again talking about lifestyle. But after all, what else is there? If I was to remain youthful, optimistic, energetic and sensual I could not stop estrogen replacement altogether. After much introspection, the decision I made was not an either/or, but a personally tailored course of action.

ESTRIOL, THE FORGOTTEN ESTROGEN?

An article I found helpful on this subject was written by Alvin H. Follingstad, M.D., more than 20 years ago and published in the Journal of the American Medical Association. It is considered groundbreaking on the subject, so I have excerpts from it below.

"There is a definite need for a safe estrogen supplement for women who are at risk of breast or endometrial carcinoma but who are denied such therapy because of recent evidence that exogenous estrogen can induce carcinoma in susceptible women. The role of supplemental estrogen in the induction of carcinoma is controversial, but the consensus is that high risk contradicts its use."

Risk Factors

"Who are the women considered to be at risk? A list of risk factors in approximate descending order of importance would be as follows: (1) previous carcinoma of breast or endometrium, with apparent long-term 'cures' or better stated, 'arrests,' (2) designated precancerous lesions combined with a strong family history of carcinoma of the breast, (3) breast- biopsy findings of a precancerous lesions such as ductal proliferation and cellular atypia, (4) mammography findings of increased density and asymmetrical density, prominent ductal pattern, diffuse punctate calcifications, and other patterns grouped under the term "dysplasia" and coupled with a positive family history, (5) a strong family history of breast cancer such as a mother and sister increasing the predicted incidence as much as fourfold, (6) severe fibrocystic disease of the breast, (7) late parity, and (8) early menarche and late menopause."

NEED FOR SUPPLEMENTS

"....the following conditions suggest the need for estrogen supplements: (1) Most authorities on the subject of severe osteoporosis agree that estrogen supplements are a necessary part of the treatment in addition to the supplements of calcium and Vitamin D and increased ambulation. M.J. Halberstam, in a recent editorial, stated that 'cancer of the endometrium is by no means a fatal disease and osteoporosis can be.' Of the estimated 4.2 million women in the United States with severe osteoporosis, 700,000 per year will suffer fractures leading to disability, deterioration, and in a substantial number, death. He believes the risks of osteoporosis far outweigh the risk of endometrial cancer. (2) Women at risk with severe menopausal symptoms are denied estrogen. (3) Young oophorectomized women are denied estrogen for the same reasons. (4) Women with treated breast or endometrial cancer and long-term arrest who suffer severe estrogen deprivation symptoms are also denied treatment using estrogen. Treated breast cancer now is an absolute contraindication for estrogen treatment.

See Halberstam, M.J. "If estrogens retard osteoporosis, are they worth the cancer risk?"

"Before going any further, it is understood that endometrial cancer is by no means the problem in frequency and mortality that is breast cancer. If diagnosed early, it is relatively easy to treat and carries a respectable cure rate. Breast cancer, on the other hand, is the leading cause of cancer death in women in the United States. Cancer of the breast will develop in one of every 15 women. Approximately 90,000 new cases are diagnosed annually, and 37,000 women per year will die of it."

THREE ACTIVE ESTROGENS

"Where does estriol fit into this problem? To understand estriol, a basic knowledge of all three active estrogens is needed. There are estrone, estradiol and estriol, which are designated in endocrinologic terminology as E1, E2 and E3, respectively. Estradiol, or E2, is the prime or true ovarian estrogen secreted by the ovary but is also found in the complex interacting biosynthesis of the body.

"Estrone, E1, is an estrogen converted from androstenedione or estradiol by biosynthesis. Androstenedione is formed in the ovary, but largely, and more importantly, by the adrenal cortex.

"Estriol, E3, although a small amount may be secreted by the ovary is converted estrogen. It is mainly converted in the liver from estrone and also by a more circuitous route from estradiol. As has been known for many years, huge amounts are secreted by the placenta, and the urinary assay of estriol in the pregnant woman has been used as an index of the viability of the fetus-falling levels indicate fetal morbidity."

"…Estrone has been thought but certainly not clinically proved, to be more carcinogenic than the more natural estradiol. The recent furor over the role of conjugated estrogens in the induction of endometrial carcinoma indicated estrone as its principal component. All present commercial and popular orally administered estrogens are estrone, combinations of estrone and estradiol, or estradiol alone. Moreover, it has been shown that orally administered estradiol, including the micronized form, is mainly converted to estrone in the small bowel, thus making all the usual orally administered estrogens, in effect, estrone. Diethylstilbestrol, now used mainly for the hormone manipulation of breast cancer, is not a steroid but is a chemical complex that acts like estrogen and is as carcinogenic as estrone.

"Parenterally administered estradiol, however, retains its identity. This should be considered when an intramuscular combination of estradiol and testosterone is chosen for a lesser carcinogenic effect…"

"Now let us look at the third and neglected estrogen, estriol. In our country it has been labeled as a weak or ineffective estrogen and difficult if not impossible to obtain."

"…There has been a growing suspicion if not a conviction that estriol may not only be noncarcinogenic but indeed anticarcinogenic. Studies of ethnic groups with low incidence of breast cancer compared with the high incidence in our country and in Britain have shown higher urinary excretion of estriol in the low-incidence countries. Animal studies have shown that a high endogenous estriol level protects against the tumor-producing effects of estrone and estradiol. A recent study shows high urinary levels of estriol related to early first-child birth and low incidence of breast cancer."

Lemon, reporting on chemically induced rat mammary carcinoma, demonstrated a notable inhibition of mammary carcinogens with estriol therapy compared with therapy using estrone and estradiol.

According to an unpublished study by Henry M. Lemon, John F. Foley and M. Anne Kessinger, 37% of participants receiving small amounts of estriol had remission or arrest of metastatic lesions.

CONCLUSION

Dr. Follingstad concludes that enough presumptive and scientific evidence has been accumulated that demonstrates orally administered estriol is safer than estrone or estradiol.

"…According to R. Philip Eaton, M.D., of the University of New Mexico School of Medicine, it is reported that protocols for clinical trials are now in progress…"

"Do we as clinicians have to wait the years necessary for the completion of these trials before estriol becomes available to us? Definitely not…enough presumptive and scientific evidence has been accumulated that we may say that orally administered estriol is safer than estrone or estradiol. The popular estrogens in use for many years can still be used for the low-risk patient, but when the high-risk patient who desperately needs estrogen for reasons already described comes to us, what shall we do? We can take the easy way and say, 'No estrogen for you.' However, if our concern leads us to take a calculated risk to stick out our necks and prescribe estrogen, let us have estrogen that causes the least risk. Let us have the opportunity of doing our own clinical trials."

Source: Alvin H. Follingstad, M.D., formerly with the Lovelace-Bataan Medical Center, Albuquerque, N.M., his article, "Estriol, the Forgotten Estrogen?" published in JAMA, Vol. 239, Issue 1, 29-30, January 2, 1978.

WEIGHT CONTROL

A clear link exists between obesity—weighing more than is appropriate for your age and height—and breast cancer. This is especially true for weight gain after menopause. Women with excess fat actually produce their own estrogen. In essence, they are replacing estrogen made from the ovaries with estrogen made from their fat tissue. Therefore, the breast is exposed to estrogen for much longer periods of time after menopause. The prolonged exposure of estrogen to the breast in these women increases their risk for breast cancer.

If women are reproducing their own estrogen from adipose tissue, why would it be dangerous? It must be bioidentical.

The only explanation I have for this dilemma is as follows: There is an extremely exquisite dance of hormones and other compounds in our bodies from birth to death. At menopause all our hormones get deregulated. Even though we may produce our own estrogen, it may be the strongest one. It is wise to keep all our hormones functioning well because, for example, DHEA (dehydroepiandrosterone), a steroid produced by the adrenal glands, converts dangerous levels of E2 into E3. As we know, E3 is the weakest of our three estrogens and has been found to protect against breast and uterine cancer. Therefore, an excess of E2 and a decrease in E3 may be the culprit involved in the contradiction above. For all intents and purposes, it is a good idea to keep our hormones balanced, our bodies and minds healthy, and practice illness prevention, not just symptom removal.

Four

EXTERNAL RISKS: RADIATION, PESTICIDES & COSMETICS

MAMMOGRAPHY

Radiologists with the encouragement of the National Cancer Institute have been urging women to have regular mammograms after the age of 40. Not everyone agrees that this is a good idea. The density of the young breast sometimes makes mammography an unreliable procedure. Dr. Steven Baum of the Long Island Jewish Hospital Medical Center has said that 99% of pre-menopausal women will have no benefit from this kind of screening.

Dr. Cornetia Barnes of the University of Toronto has gone further, saying, "We will not say that mammography kills. The conclusion that will be reached is that younger women do not benefit." Dr. William Campbell Douglass Jr., an alternative therapy physician and publisher of *The Douglass Report*, warns against questionable amounts of compression to the breast and repeated doses of radiation.

I say mammograms can kill when they instill a false sense of security in women. Almost, all women I talked to believe they are home free if they have their yearly mammogram. As I mentioned earlier, Dr. Gamagami told me my mammogram was perfect. At the time of that test, I had invasive breast cancer the mammogram did not detect. If I had not insisted I felt a lump and asked for further testing, my prognosis would not have been the same.

What's to be done? Remember, mammograms show calcifications and abnormal architectural charges.

Not all tumors are associated with obvious suspicious calcifications or architectural distortion that can be clearly seen on a mammogram. It is estimated that 15 to 20% of breast cancers are missed by mammography. However, in some instances early changes of cancer such as small areas of calcification can be seen on a mammogram and the tumor may be detected before it can be felt. In this instance mammography can be lifesaving.

Many physicians today believe that digital mammography is a superior tool for seeing the breast detail. In patients with dense breasts, ultrasound can complement mammography in sometimes identifying tumors not seen on a mammogram. In addition, ultrasound can increase the likelihood of finding a cancer when combined with mammography. However, it is not a substitute for mammography as it does not show calcifications and certain other changes seen on mammograms.

MRI is considered by many to be the best imaging tool for finding breast cancer. Its current major drawback is considered to be the fact that it will also call many benign lesions suspicious. As a result, unnecessary biopsies may be performed. Nevertheless, this tool may be especially appropriate for higher risk individuals with dense breasts that are difficult to visualize by mammography.

You and your doctor must decide upon the frequency of your screening and the most appropriate studies to follow your breasts. This will be influenced by your age, breast consistency, personal and family history, and other risk factors.

X-RAY HAZARDS

Many people instinctually back away from an X-ray machine and do not stay in the same room with their children when they are X-rayed. Why do we do this??? Because we all know radiation exposure is not good for you.

Every time I express a concern over X-ray exposure the technician or doctor will assure me the risk is miniscule. The problem with their reassurances is neither of them know how many

X-rays or scans I have already had. When you fill out the paper-work in a doctor's office, he or she is very certain to ask you about all your previous surgeries and the medications you are taking. Never has a doctor asked about an X-ray or scan diary to ascertain the amount of radiation I have had. Now that I am in my 50s, they are even less concerned. Why is that? If a person gets exposed to a carcinogen it takes usually 20 or 30 years to cause the cancer. It is assumed that if I were to get an overdose of radiation from scans at this age, I would not manifest the fatal disease until my 70s or 80s. Somehow this information is not comforting. Most of us would agree that we would rather die in our sleep in our 90s!

CT Scans

I became even more concerned after reading a September 7, 2008, article in the *Los Angeles Times*, "Revolutionary (CT) Scans Come With a Risk."

The article explained that computed tomography (CT) scans were introduced in the 1970s and have become a standard procedure, with U.S. doctors ordering 68.7 million CT scans [in 2007], more than triple the number in 1995!

The article went on to explain that this increase is causing rising concern that more frequent use of radiation is having an effect on the health of our nation. The article cited a study published in the New England Journal of Medicine estimating that CT scans administered today could cause up to 2% of cancer deaths in two or three decades. I believe that even a tiny increase in radiation exposure spread over a large population can add up to tens of thousands of cancer deaths every year.

CANCER RISK

The article also explained how CT scans can create cancer risks when:

- Radiation loosens an electron from an atom which creates an ion that damages a cell's DNA.

- Irradiated cells typically die, but if the dose of radiation damage is sufficient to kill the cell, the damaged cell may divide and multiply over time, spreading the faulty genetic information.

"The result is cancer," the article concluded.

"The best data on low-level radiation exposure comes from studies of about 25,000 survivors from two or three miles outside the blast zone of the Hiroshima and Nagasaki atomic bombs at the end of WWII. They received between 5 and 150 millisieverts—the equivalent of a few CT scans—and small but statistically significant increase in cancer and death rates according to studies," the article also said.

Even scarier was what followed: a conclusion by the National Academy of Sciences that no safe level of radiation exposure exists and that even small doses pose some health risks.

CT scans have become an economic consideration for doctors and hospitals, the article continued, with Siemens and General Electric Company promoting their easy profitability. Two scans a day can pay for the device in five years. Ten scans a day can bring in more than $400,000 a year profit, according to the Times article.

"Patients come in with a headache," Dr. Scott Lederhaus, a neurosurgeon in Pomona, was quoted in the article. "If they don't get scanned and something gets missed, they can sue. So I order the scan, it's not worth the aggravation."

"Since doctors have been suffering as the dollars and cents are being squeezed out of a medical practice, why shouldn't they get their own equipment?" Dr. Madyoon, another cardiologist in the article, noted. "You've got to survive."

A report by the U.S. Government Accountability Office suggested that financial concerns for doctors were a major factor in the rising number of CT scans. It is natural for a doctor to use machines they purchased or have some stake in. These doctors are two to seven times more likely to order tests than other doctors who made referrals to outside facilities.

The standard unit of measure for radiation dose exposure is millisieverts. A CT scan delivers a dose of 5 to 25 millisieverts. The United States limits public exposure to 1 millisievert per year although 50 millisieverts is the allowable exposure for those working in radiation environments. According to the Times article, one doctor who surveyed records for an imaging company discovered that 11,535 patients had received more than 50 millisieverts from CT scans, 107 patients had received more than 200 millisieverts and one poor soul got 992 millisieverts!

After doing the research, I began thinking about all the X-rays and scans that I have had. Every one of those times I was reassured that the radiation dose was nothing to worry about.

A CT scan of my left axilla to image a swollen lymph node, a complete bone scan with radioactive isotopes to rule out bone cancer. I was having aches and pains in my joints from fibromyalgia, so, a complete body scan. Remember when they were all the rage?? The tech actually told me that all of the employees in the office were going to have one every year.

I also had a CT scan of my lungs just a year ago because my gynecologist suggested I have my lungs checked out because of my age. Now I realize because of my age, that a CT scan actually could have started a lung cancer in progress.

I was given a barium enema to view my large intestine because I have a family history of polyps. I read that one researcher concluded there are higher cancer risks attributed to barium enemas. We know I had breast cancer at the time of that scan, did that have anything to do with its spread??? Young girls who have had chest X-rays for lung infections have a higher risk later in life to develop breast cancer, some doctors say.

I can't go back and undo what has been done, but I am wiser now. I will always be hyper vigilant about CT scans in the future and have one only if it is truly necessary

Further, with digital mammography centers, there are new options on the table now. We can decrease radiation to our breasts and that is a good thing!

PESTICIDES

"Breast cancer incidence may be linked to both pesticide exposure and overuse of antibiotics. Until further studies are conducted and more is known about these possible links, be cautious. Also be aware of how these substances might counterbalance your efforts at breast cancer prevention."

"Researchers have learned that women with elevated levels of pesticides in their breast tissue have a greater breast cancer risk."

Source: Mayo Clinic, "Breast Cancer Prevention: Lifestyle Factors that Can Reduce Risk," MayoClinic.com.

Many pesticides including malathion and parathion are members of the nerve gas family.

"So lethal is parathion that a chemist who swallowed an infinitesimal dose, amounting to 0.00424 of an ounce, was instantaneously paralyzed and died before he could take an antidote he had prepared in advance and had at hand," reported John Robbins in his book, *Diet for a New America.*

How many of you believe that washing your fruits and vegetables keeps you safe from pesticides??? Do you know most pesticides in the diet come from meat and dairy? How many moms wash the apples they give to their youngsters and then serve them a large glass of pesticide-laden milk? How does this happen?

"Cows are kept in deplorable farm conditions. They are so filthy and crowded together that the animals get sick. Then they are given antibiotics and dipped in a bath of toxic pesticides.

These pesticides are retained in the fat of the animal. The cows become carriers of the most deadly chemicals ever known," Robbins wrote.

The Pesticides Monitoring Journal published by the EPA from 1967 to 1981, chronicled scientific studies and research findings regarding these toxins.

"Foods of animal origins are the major source of pesticides that reside in the American diet," Robbins says.

If you want to include pesticides in your diet eat meat, poultry, fish, dairy and eggs. While most of us have heard about DDT, many other toxic chemicals exist that are equally widespread and actually more poisonous The pesticide, dieldrin is five times more poisonous than DDT and 40 times more when absorbed by the skin. By the time dieldrin was banned in 1974 the FDA found it in96% of all meat, fish, and poultry in the country ; in 85% of all dairy products; and in the flesh of 99.5% of all American people. Dieldrin will be with us for many decades because it takes that long to break it down.

Dioxin is "by far the most toxic chemical know to mankind," according to Dr. Diane Courtney, the former head of the Toxic Effects Branch of the EPA's National Center for Environmental Research Center.

Dioxin is actually not one chemical but a general term describing hundreds of chemicals with long technical names that, once they enter the environment, animals and people, persist for years. It is created as a manufacturing by-product from processes such as waste incineration, chemical and pesticide manufacturing, and pulp and paper bleaching.

Courtney testified years ago that dioxin is present in beef and dairy products from cattle that have grazed on land treated with 2,4,5-T. , an herbicide whose impurities include dioxin. Because of the dangers associated with the herbicide, it was phased out in 1985 by the U.S. Department of Agriculture.

"Millions of pounds of this lethal chemical have been sprayed on land in the United States. Since dioxin is stored and concentrated as it moves up the food chain, cows, pigs and chickens contain in their flesh the dioxin residues from all the plants they have ever eaten," says John Robbins, author and founder of EarthSave, an organization dedicated to encouraging people to shift to a plant-based diet.

"Humans who eat beef…can get a concentrated dose of dioxin that has built up for several years," says Lewis Regenstein, author of *How to Survive in America the Poisoned.*

Dioxin causes cancer, birth defects, miscarriages and death in lab animals at the lowest possible levels to test---one part per trillion.

HEPTACHOR STRIKES IN THE SOUTH

Several years after the insecticide heptachor was finally restricted, the Department of Agriculture discovered that as part of its school lunch program, it had sent 40,000 pounds. of heptachlor-contaminated ground pork to school systems in Louisiana and Arkansas. By the time they realized what had been done, over 14,000 pounds. of poisoned pork had been consumed by the children.

The problem with pesticides is the damage and havoc they create has a lag time. When we eat bacteria we get sick immediately: cramps, vomiting and fever. When we eat pesticides they gradually accumulate over time and then we get the chilling effects such as cancer and birth defects many years later.

PCB's

Monsanto Corporation first produced PCBs (polychlorinated biphenyls) in the United States in the 1930s. They were used to manufacture less flammable cooling and insulating fluids for industrial transformers and capacitors and flexible coatings for electrical wiring and electronic components. Monsanto had a motto, "Without chemicals Life itself would be Impossible".

Not long after PCBs were introduced it became apparent these chemicals posed major problems for human beings.

"Three years after production began, the faces and bodies of 23 out of 24 workers in the Monsanto plant became disfigured. But that didn't stop Monsanto; since then more than 750,000 tons of these deadly poisons have been produced. They can be found today in every river in America, the snow in the Arctic and Antarctica, and probably the tissues in every single fish in the waters of this planet," writes John Robbins.

So there you have it. We eat the fish, we get PCB's. We eat the beef, we get dosed with dioxin, We eat the pork, we get heptachor poisoning. And all the time the government is reassuring us our food supply is safe!

Even when these pesticides are banned in the United States, they are then sold to third-world countries. These countries use these dangerous chemicals on their products and then we import their beef for our fast food restaurants.

"We have the dubious distinction of being the worlds' largest producer of pesticides. We use 1.1 billion pounds of pesticides a year—about five pounds for every member of the population," writes John Robbins.

Even mother's milk is contaminated with dangerous pesticides. Is there any wonder why immune system disorders and cancer are out of control? What can be done?

Minimize your intake of meat, fish, dairy products and eggs. Choose organic produce. Reduce your intake of imported foods, like coffee, sugar, tea and bananas, because farmers in other countries such as Costa Rica, Ecuador, Guatemala and Mexico use much greater concentrations of pesticides than even American agriculture allows. Choose in-season, locally grown fruits and vegetables. And remember, the worst of all foods are fast food hamburgers, because they are often made from beef imported from Central America.

I recommend the book by John Robbins' *Diet for a New America* if you want to learn more about your food supply.

TOXIC LOTIONS AND POTIONS

How many of you believe your cosmetics are safe? The FDA must be on top of poisons in our potions, wouldn't you think? Well, think again; a little known fact is that there are only **ten** ingredients banned from cosmetics in the United States. Ingredients banned from cosmetics in the European Union number over **one thousand** ...shocking.... hair raising!

Every day many of us use multiple "beauty products," starting with our shampoo, deodorant, moisture lotion, and finally, makeup. We sometimes think that expensive products are made from superior ingredients. That is not necessarily true. My favorite Chanel lipstick rated a 6 on a scale from 1 to 10, with 10 being most toxic; that is not good. Literally, I was ingesting this almost every day. I remember a few years back I saw a curious picture in a magazine. It was a soup bowl full of broken lipsticks floating around in it. I thought at the time, it was interesting. I recognized the fact we ingest our lipsticks, but I didn't realize how toxic they might be. Revlon lipsticks scored the unspeakable number 9 on the toxicity chart. That is like putting poison on your lips every day.

According to Skin Deep, an online cosmetic safety database maintained by the nonprofit Environmental Working Group, all cosmetics can be rated from 0-10, with 0-2, low hazard, 3-6 moderate, and 7-10 high risk.

Every time our bottle of liquid makeup runs dry we run to purchase another one. Where does that stuff go? The skin drinks it and it enters our bodies so it's not surprising harmful chemicals have gotten into our breast milk and children as well. These chemicals cause cancer, birth defects, learning disabilities and a host of other health problems that plague our society today.

The cosmetics industry assures us that the toxins in our cosmetics are safe, but since "there is no government standard for safety, companies can say whatever they want about the safety of their products," according to The Campaign for Safe Cosmetics. The cosmetics industry says the amounts are allowable and small. Yet, most of us ladies use many products every day. Over time, the cumulative exposure builds up and can result in illness.

According to Skin Deep, product categories of highest concern are: hair color, hair bleach, hair relaxer, nail polish and skin lighteners. A word about skin lighteners: Many dermatologists give their patients hydroquinone for brown spots; but just because many do so does not make it safe. As a matter of fact, hydroquinone is a possible carcinogen and probable neurotoxin, and can also cause irreversible skin disease.

Some chemicals that are known to be toxic but are still in our cosmetics: Mercury is in eye drops and mascara, lead in hair dyes and cleaners, and 1,4-dioxane, from the breakdown of petrochemicals such as mineral oil, paraffin and petroleum, is found in hair relaxers, antiaging creams, perfumes, makeup foundations, lipstick and lip balm. Nanoparticles of these harmful substances are capable of being absorbed directly into the bloodstream from eye shadows, bronzers, sunscreens and lotions.

The word "natural" is no guarantee the product is safe. According to *Skin Deep*, Neutrogena's After-Sun Treatment with natural soy has one of the highest hazard ratings of the lotions tested. Neutrogena, owned by the global corporation, Johnson & Johnson, markets its products as superior because of their "natural" ingredients and recommendations from health-care providers.

I was using a Neutrogena product myself. I thought it was a good product because it was recommended by the American Cancer Society. The product I was using, Neutrogena Ultra Sheer Dry-Touch Sunblock SPF 55, scored a 7, equally a health hazard. How ironic, a product that is pricey, feels good on the skin and is recommended by the American Cancer Society is toxic!

The American Cancer Society evaluated the product from a UVA and UVB perspective. It does block harmful sunrays, which helps prevent skin cancer and melanoma. But the big picture is not good. Ingredients in this sunscreen have raised concerns about reproductive toxicity, allergy/immune toxicity, endocrine disruption, bioaccumulation, organ system toxicity, and irritation to skin, eyes or lungs. I stopped using the product immediately and returned it to the pharmacy where I purchased it. I began to see how all the lotions and potions I was using were like taking liquid gels of them daily. We all know these products are for external use only. Now, we know they enter our skin as surely as if we had swallowed them…uck!! A list of some of the things I was using may interest you. It certainly got my attention when I saw the toxicity numbers, according to Skin Deep.

Product	Toxicity Rating
Neutrogena Ultra Sheer Dry Touch Sunblock, SPF 55	*7*
MD Skincare All-In-One Tinted Moisturizer, SPF 15	*4*
Lancome Black "Hypnose" Mascara	*4*
Chanel Aqua Lumiere Lipstick	*6*
Vaseline Intensive Care Rescue Moisture Lotion	*8*
Neutrogena Sunless Tanning Foam	*5*
MAC Matte Lipstick	*3*
Neutrogena Body Oil	*4*
MAC Under Eye Concealer	*3*
Lubriderm Advanced Therapy Creamy Body Lotion	*8*

I was using several products a day and not one of them was in the low hazard zone of 0-2!!!

A 2007 study by the Environmental Working Group, (EWG) revealed that 22 % of all cosmetics may be contaminated with a cancer-causing impurity. The results of this chemical safety assessment of cosmetics found common petroleum-based cosmetic ingredients can contain the carcinogen 1, 4-dioxane. This chemical is easily absorbed by the skin, leaving consumers at risk for potential chronic and widespread exposure to this cancer-causing compound. Futhermore, this chemical has been found in 15 products for babies and children. Since we know these toxins can accumulate over time, why would the government allow them in products for babies and young children?

The answer is, the cosmetics industry has been left to "police itself. It does this through a "safety panel" that is run and funded by the industry's trade association. It is never a good idea to let any organization police itself. To say the results will be skewed towards the outcome they want is an understatement. Until the FDA comes down hard on the cosmetics industry, as I believe they should, it is prudent to choose your products carefully.

With the power of information comes responsibility. Check your cosmetics on EWG's online database, Skin Deep, www.cosmeticsdatabase.com.

And be well.

CANDLES AND AIR FRESHENERS

Guess what? Your run-of-the-mill paraffin-based candles are toxic. The by-products of burning paraffin with lead wicks are carcinogenic. Just as you thought you knew so much about what's healthful and what's not, here is another concern! Once you burn paraffin it releases carcinogenic toxins such as benzene and toluene.

Don't despair; there are alternatives for those spa enthusiasts that love the ambiance of candlelight when bathing, dining or just about anything else.

BURNING SOY

"Add a calm glow and an eco-chic sensibility with 100% soy candles…" (Myron Mariano, Organic Magazine, January/February 2009). Make the switch to soy candles, here's why:

Because they are green, a renewable resource rather than a petroleum-based product.

Because they double as massage oil, melted soy wax works as a fantastic moisturizer as well as soothing massage oil, because it doesn't firm back up when removed from the heat source.

Because they burn better, "clean burning soy leaves minimal wax residue and won't produce the petroleum-based paraffin black soot residue know as 'ghosting' on furnishing or walls," explains the creator of Verikira Nauturals, Kira Peterson. "Soy is less likely to trigger allergy problems than paraffin. Also, the wicks of our green candles are made without the harmful lead."

Because they support the community, "we are passionate about supporting American farmers…businesses and Mother Nature as we are about candles and that's the way we think it ought to be," says Karen Schmacher, founder of Heirloom Candles.

Because they last longer, "soy is a biodegradable and water soluble product that burns cooler than paraffin and, therefore, slower," says Christine White-Stanton of Scandle Candles.

Beeswax candles are not only beautiful to look at, they are a safe alternative to paraffin-based candles. Beeswax candles are green and as wonderful to use as soy.

Simply Organics beeswax candles cause no asthma, allergies or headaches; the same can't be said for the toxins produced by paraffin-based candles. Cost $28.00.

So, take all your gorgeous, pretty smelling and probably expensive paraffin candles out to the patio and use them there. Then, replace paraffin with beeswax or soy for your interior. Create a beautiful ambiance in your home without the fear of compromising your health.

Before the party, beware of fragrances. Most fragrances we are used to smelling in household air fresheners contain formaldehyde and all kinds of toxins. Use essential oils, they provide a more natural scent without chemicals. You can find a variety of scents from places like The Body Shop and Whole Foods. Now, go have a green party!

SECTION III

PREVENTION

Five

Food for Health

As a preface to this chapter, I would like to call your attention to the following: Parenthesis or an asterisk (*) at the end of each sentence indicates direct quotes reprinted from The Doctor's Book of Food Remedies, Copyright (1998) by Selene Yeager and editors of Prevention magazine. Permission granted by Rodale, Inc. Emmaus, PA 18098.

The information contained in this chapter is extensive but not totally exhaustive. I would encourage you to read The Doctor's Book of Food Remedies on your own to get more useful facts that will help you with your quest for good health.

Breast Cancer Defense

"One of the best defenses against breast cancer may well be diet! A growing and impressive body of research reveals that what you eat and drink can help protect you against disease."

Source: Andrew Weil, M.D., author and leader in integrative medicine.

This chapter begins the third and final section of my book, "Prevention." This chapter deals with health-giving food. In subsequent chapters, I focus on herbs, medical practices you should follow, and personal regimens like yoga, massage and stress relief that can help prevent illness. I hope the information I have collected will impart knowledge to enable all of you to live healthier and happier lives.

Let's start with one of the basic ways to maintain health: minimizing the inflammatory response of your body. Recent studies have shown that the inflammatory response by the body creates a host of major problems and diseases. That is why it is very important to ingest foods and herbs that are anti-inflammatory, these substances calm the inflammation process that occurs naturally in our bodies. Also, any substance that protects our DNA from damage The markers for inflammation—substances whose levels would indicate that the inflammatory response in our bodies is high—are nitric oxide, C-reactive protein and T cell activation.

"Inflammation can occur from ingesting sugars cooked with proteins and fats, as in the browning of foods. This yields substances called advanced glycation end products (AGEs). When consumed, AGEs create oxidative damage to the body and cause extra inflammation. Meat cooked at high temperature, processed foods and full-fat cheese have high AGE levels, but fruits and vegetables, whole grains and low- fat dairy products are low in AGEs." *

That is why it is very important to ingest foods and herbs that are anti-inflammatory These substances calm the inflammation process that occurs naturally in our bodies. "In addition, any substance that protects our DNA from damage is a lifesaver. These lifesavers are called antioxidants. Their official names are polyphenols and carotenoids, found in many fruits and vegetables. By protecting against damage to DNA, we block a trigger that promotes cancer growth." *

One study found that breast cancer patients with the highest levels of carotenoids had a 43% lower risk of breast cancer recurrence compared to women with the lowest carotenoid levels.

Source: Journal of Clinical Oncology, *September 2005.*

From "a to z" in the following list, I hope to show you the health benefits of everyday foods in your diet.

"**Barley** contains lignans, a powerful antioxidant. Eating lots of it can reduce the risk of breast cancer by nearly 34%."*

"**Basil** not only prevents cancer it eases digestion and is a good remedy for gas. That is because it contains eugenol, also known as clove oil." *

Beans are a fiber-rich protein and antioxidant abundant. Beans keep blood sugar steady. They also have been shown to inhibit cancer-cell growth.

"**Beets** contain betacyanins and betaxanthins, which are generous donors of electrons that neutralize free radicals. Beets inhibit growth of breast, stomach, colon, lung and nervous system tumor cells." *

Berries are full of ellagic acid, which helps fight cancer by its powerful antioxidant properties.

Broccoli is the cream of crucifers, containing Carbon13 (13C) and sulforaphane which sweep for cancer-causing substances.

Also in this category are **Brussels sprouts, cabbage, cauliflower** and **bok choy.** These are powerful vegetables that fight cancer. Try to eat one at least once a day. If that's not possible, Dr. Reiss has a supplement that works in the body as if you were ingesting cruciferous vegetables.

"**Indoles,** organic compounds found in broccoli and cabbage, are equivalent to Carbon 13. 13C is able to knock down harmful forms of estrogen while increasing more benign forms of the hormone." * Therefore, if a woman has had breast cancer, a healthy dose of 13C every day is recommended.

"**Cabbage** contains glutamine, an amino acid that increases blood flow to the stomach, thereby strengthening its protective lining and helping prevent ulcers. Don't cook the cabbage; heat will destroy its anti-ulcer abilities." *

"**Cartenoids** fight cancer, they are also good for your eyes. Examples of carotenoid-rich foods include cantaloupe, carrots, kale, oranges, peaches, pumpkin, sweet potatoes, spinach and tomatoes." *

"**Celery** is a member of the parsley family. The leaves have the most nutrients, which contain coumarins. Coumarins stop free radicals. Celery leaves also contain acetylenics, which stop tumor growth, and phenolic acid which blocks prostaglandins which can cause inflammation. So eat your celery!" *

Cherries relieve gout and taste good, too, most of us know. But I did not know they contain perillyl alcohol, which cures mammary cancer in rats. Also, they contain quercetin which blocks free radicals and reduces arthritis inflammation. I will be pointing out many foods that contain quercetin, because this substance is so important for our fight against cancer.

Cinnamon improves the body's ability to utilize insulin and absorb glucose.

"**Cloves** contain eugenol, a numbing compound. West African black pepper, which contains eugenol, appears to produce changes in the brains of mice that reduce the severity of seizures." *

"**Coffee** reduces the risk of cancer while increasing mood and alertness. Coffee contains polyphenols that work their magic against the disease. The risk of cancer decreased with an increase in the amount of coffee each day. Both regular and decaf have the same properties, according to one study in lung cancer patients." *

Cranberries and **blueberries** are extremely high in antidioxdants such as ellagic acid. Ellagic acid has caused high hopes in cancer researchers. Cranberries have been shown to protect against breast, colon, prostate, head and neck cancers. "Cranberries also contain quercetin, myricetin and kaempferol, which prevent genetic changes from cancer." * So, find some time to eat your cranberries.

"**Fish** protects against breast cancer in two specific ways. First, it supplies a lot of the Omega-3 fatty acids, which metabolize dangerous hormones into the safer 2-hydroxyestrone form. Second, fish oil contains Vitamin D which has been shown to lower your cancer risk overall. Be sure to choose fish that are low in mercury! If you don't like fish, then supplement with fish oil capsules." *

"**Flavonoids** are in tea, dark chocolate, cranberries, grapes, strawberries and other fruits and vegetables. They prevent heart disease and the growth of cancer, plus, improve brain function." *

Flaxseed contains lignans, estrogenlike chemicals that protect against free radicals. "Lignans also subdue cancerous changes once they have occurred, rendering them less likely to race out of control and develop into full-blown cancer." * Dr. Andrew Weil recommends using flaxseeds rather than supplementing with flax oil. "The oil typically lacks the beneficial lignans and fiber," states Dr. Weil.

Garlic stimulates the immune system. Most of us know that garlic is very healthy, but we say it's too smelly and strong. I suggest roasting the garlic wrapped in aluminum foil in the oven at 350 degrees for 45 minutes, or microwaving on high for 10 minutes and turning twice.

Ginger helps prevent the production of prostaglandins, compounds that cause pain and swelling (inflammation). Simply place three or four slices of ginger in a cup of boiling water, then enjoy your drink. Not only is ginger good for inflammation reduction, it is excellent for stomach upset. I try to have fresh ginger root in the house at all times.

"Ginger's health benefits are the result of gingerol, which reduces inflammation associated with arthritis. Those that suffer osteo and rheumatoid arthritis will have less pain. Gingerol relaxes blood vessels that cause nausea and vomiting. This is why ginger is also good for motion sickness." *

Grape juice gives you the health benefits of red wine (see Wine) without the alcohol, and it tastes good, too.

Red grapefruit is healthier than white. It contains lycopene, limonoids and naringin. These compounds protect the heart and decrease the risk of cancer.

Green tea, a tonic for you and me, is loaded with antioxidants. A recent analysis of data found that drinking five cups of green tea a day reduces breast cancer risk by 22% (Carcinogenesis, July 2006). Dr. Weil recommends at least one cup a day.

Greens protect against cancer and also help vision. Iceberg lettuce is the least nutritious of the bunch. Better choices include beet greens, dandelion, kale, spinach, Swiss chard and turnip greens. Beet greens and spinach are rich sources of riboflavin, a B vitamin that is essential for tissue growth and repair.

"**Guavas** are rich in lycopene, a healthy fat-soluble compound. One Israeli study found guavas block the growth of lung and breast cancer cells. One guava fruit contains nine grams of fiber per cup!" *

"**Isothiocyanates** (mustard oils) have been found in broccoli, cabbage and Brussels sprouts. Isothiocyanates show promise for preventing cancer." *

"**Lemons and limes** heal cuts and bruises, prevent cancer and heart disease. Limonin and limonene, two compounds in these fruits, appear to help block some cellular changes that lead to cancer. Also, limonin helps eliminate estradiol, a naturally occurring hormone that has been linked with breast cancer." *

"**Lignans** are plant estrogens. Lignans keep levels of human estrogen in check. Examples are flaxseed, broccoli, apricots, kale, cabbage and strawberries." *

"**Mango** extract inhibited the growth of cancer cells in test tubes. They are also rich in fiber; one mango equals seven grams of fiber." *

"**Melons**, especially cantaloupes, are healthful. They are full of folate, a water-soluble B vitamin which has been shown to reduce the risk of polyps, precancerous growth in the colon." *

"**Monoterpenses**, components found in the essential oils of citrus fruits, are equivalent to limonene. Limonene is a soldier in the battle against cancer. This very important substance can be found in orange and lemon peels. These citrus oils actually were found to shrink breast tumors. Monoterpenses are also found in cherries in the form of perillyl alcohol and has been shown to prevent cancer of the breast, lung, stomach, liver and skin." * Now, that's what I'm talking about!

Mushrooms, the fabulous fungus! "Mushrooms inhibit tumor growth, boost immune system and lower cholesterol. American's favorite mushroom, the white button, packs quite a punch especially when it comes to preventing breast cancer. Mushrooms suppress estrogen, particularly in postmenopausal women. Mice fed mushroom extract had a 58% reduction in growth of breast tumors. Mushrooms contain linoleic acid, which inhibits aromatase, the protein in the body that makes estrogen. As for shitake and maitake mushrooms, shitake have long been used in Japan to shrink tumors and maitake mushrooms have a polysaccaride called beta-glucan or D-fraction, which shrinks tumors in lab animals. But do not eat mushrooms raw. They contain hydrazine, a compound with toxic chemicals that produce tumors. Always cook your mushrooms to eliminate hydrazines." *

"**Oats** mop up cholesterol, reduce heart disease, lower blood sugar and fight cancer. Oats contain generous amounts of phytic acid, which binds with reactive minerals that may be important in the prevention of colon cancer. Also the high fiber in oats lowers risk for cancer." *

"**Olive oil** provides help for the heart because it lowers cholesterol and reduces the risk of heart disease, as well as breast cancer and rheumatoid arthritis. Experts believe extra virgin olive oil reduces the risk of rheumatoid arthritis because of its anti-inflammatory effects. One study found that the oil was similar to ibuprofen in reducing inflammation. Light olive oil also stands up to heat well, so you can use it for high heat frying. As documented by a Greek study, women who ate olive oil more than once a day had a 25% lower risk of breast cancer." *

Onions and garlic contain allylic sulfides. They are smelly stuff that makes good sense to eat because of their toxin-eliminating enzymes. They are particularly effective against cancers of the gastrointestinal tract. "They make cancer self-destruct in a process called apoptosis. Also allicin, an organic compound in garlic, is a potent germ killer. Garlic juice has been found to kill antibiotic resistant strains of highly infectious staph bacteria." *

Onions are part of the allium family; they lower blood pressure, decrease cancer risk, reduce congestion and inflammatory processes. They contain quercetin, which fights free radicals. Also, "onions contain sulfur compounds that lower triglycerides, the chemical form in which most fat exists in the body, and keeps breathing passages free and clear." * So, therefore, I suggest you eat your onions and carry your Altoids!

"**Oranges** lower the risk of heart disease and fight cancer. Oranges are the perfect fruit. They contain Vitamin C, fiber and natural sugar for energy, as well as limonin and hesperidin. Limonin and hesperidin show a lot of promise for blocking cancer. Hesperidin stops inflammation. Vitamin C and limonin get cancer cells to self-destruct!" *

"**Papayas** have carotenoids, an extremely powerful antidioxidant. They also contain papain, an enzyme, which aides in digestion. A Russian study found papaya speeds wound healing!" *

Red-hot paprika is an anti-inflammatory and antioxidant agent.

"**Peas**, the little green mean machine, contain chlorophyllin, which has a special molecular shape that allows it to grab cancer-causing chemicals in the body. Peas are a legume; one-half cup equals as much protein as a tablespoon of peanut butter without the fat." *

Phytonutrients have antioxidant abilities. Many diseases and aging are caused by free radical damage. When you eat broccoli or other fresh vegetables some of the phytonutrients begin stomping out the enemy.

Pineapple keeps bones strong, improves digestion, and relieves cold symptoms. But the big one is that pineapple eases inflammation. We know we always want to keep our body's inflammatory process in check! "Pineapple eases the inflammation and swelling of rheumatoid arthritis, tendonitis, bursitis, soft tissue injury and even chronic pain. Bromelin, an enzyme in pineapple, also speeds healing after surgery." * This is an important issue for cancer survivors.

Pomegranate, according to *The Doctor's Book of Food Remedies*, "prostate cancer survivors and men at risk should sip eight ounces of 100% pomegranate juice a day. Pomegranate changes the way prostate cancer grows and slows the rise of prostate biomarkers." *

"**Potatoes** with their skins contain Vitamin C, B6, copper, manganese, potassium and seven grams of fiber. The potato peel specifically contains chlorogenic acid, which absorbs benzopyrene, a potential carcinogen found in smoked foods. So be sure to have your potato skins with your grilled hamburgers." *

"**Prunes** relieve constipation, lower cholesterol and reduce the risk of cancer and heart disease. Five prunes a day will do it! Prunes have the health-giving compound, betacarotene, and are fiber rich. Whole prunes are better for constipation than juice." *

"**Pumpkin** provides potent protection, because it contains betacarotene, lutein and zeaxanthin, which are very effective, free radical scavengers. Pumpkin lowers the risk of lung cancer and is iron rich. Pumpkin is also good for brittle bones because of its zinc content." * So it seems that Peter, Peter the pumpkin eater knew what he was doing!

Pectin provides water-soluble fiber that binds to potentially harmful substances, thus preventing them from being absorbed by the body. Examples of fruits that contain pectin are apples, grapefruit, bananas, peaches and also beans. It seems that an apple a day may keep the doctor away.

"**Raisins** are a low-fat, high-energy food and fiber rich. Raisins contain ample amounts of potassium, which is important for heart health. Catechins, the same compounds found in green tea, are also in raisins and were found to reduce intestinal tumors by at least 70% in lab mice. Other studies found that the fiber and tartaric acid play an important role in colon health. For those of you that are anemic, raisins are an excellent source of iron." *

"**Rhubarb,** a member of the buckwheat family, is fiber rich, relieving constipation as it flushes out cholesterol. Vitamin C and rhubarb juice rank high in the ability to prevent cell mutations, which cause cancer." *

Rice as we all know, is most nutritious when it is brown. Brown rice contains abundant amounts of fiber, complex carbohydrates and essential B vitamins. "Brown rice contains oryzanol, which reduces the body's production of cholesterol. Brown rice has a lot of insoluble fiber that can reduce the risk of colon cancer." *

What's good for the colon is good for the breast. The fiber in brown rice binds with estrogen in the digestive tract creating less available hormones in the bloodstream.

"**Raspberries, mulberries** and **peanuts** starve cancer cells by interfering with a protein called nuclear factor-kappa beta that helps feed them." *

"**Safer Grilling** methods reduce your exposure to carciogens. Overcooking to the point of well done transforms compounds in meat, poultry and fish into cancer-causing chemicals called hetero-cyclic amines. Therefore, marinate your meat and chicken; it makes it less carcinogenic." * Also don't eat the burned parts of the meat whenever possible and buy free-range and grass-fed organic products.

"**Saponins,** a class of chemical compounds, stimulate the immune system. Saponins are found in beans, spinach, tomatoes, potatoes, nuts, legumes and oats. People who eat these have lower rates of breast, prostate and colon cancer. They work by binding with bilic acids, which over time may metabolize into cancer-causing compounds. Another process by which they work is by targeting the cancer-causing cholesterol in cancer cell membranes." *

"**Sea vegetables**, such as kelp and dulse, inhibit tumor growth, boost immunity and prevent macular degeneration. Kelp and dulse have been reported to reduce the risk of mammary cancer in animal studies." *

Soy helps ward off breast cancer, which is estrogen driven, by blocking estrogen receptors. Soy products contain weak plant estrogens that displace estradiol, your body's most potent form of the hormone. Something I did not know is that only one-third of Americans can metabolize soy into a form associated with greater risk reduction. Therefore, this topic remains controversial. "If your cancer is estrogen positive and you're taking tamoxifen, you should consult with your oncologist before consuming soy products," suggests Dr. Weil.

Spices are special flavorings that contain healing potential. Examples are black pepper, cumin, cloves, cinnamon, nutmeg, fenugreek and turmeric. Turmeric is a warrior in the fight against cancer. "Turmeric is being intensely studied for its anti-inflammatory and cancerprotective effects. With evidence growing for the health benefits of curcumin, turmeric's best-known active ingredient, I suggest jazzing up the cooking with the spice," states Dr. Weil. For those who do not like the taste of this pungent spice, an alternative is to take a curcumin supplement such as Turmeric Force or in tea form. But beware: Too much curcumin could raise your bleeding risk.

"Nutmeg, ginger, cumin, black pepper and coriander block atatoxin, a mold that can cause liver cancer. Saffron is capable of killing human cancer cells. Saffron also protects against cataracts, lowers triglycerides and prevents excessive blood clotting." *

"**Squash** prevents lung problems and reduces the risk of endometrial cancer. For people with asthma, squash is rich in Vitamin C, which lowers the occurrence of lung problems. Beta-carotene reduces risk of endometrial cancer. Also, squash has betaxanthins, which have been shown to cut lung cancer by 2% to 37%. The Vitamin A, potassium and folate in squash help lower homocysteine, an amino acid, which, if found at high levels in the blood, can lead to higher risk of heart disease, stroke and peripheral vascular disease." * I saw a segment of the Rachel Ray cooking show recently in which she cooked spaghetti squash instead of the pasta. She dressed the squash with sauce, cheese and basil. It looked really tasty. I think I will try it, will you?

Stress is the enemy. Chronic stress knocks down your defenses, both physically and psychologically. Therefore, breathe and don't wait to exhale. B vitamins help ease stress. Carbohydrates such as pasta, bagels and potatoes can raise your levels of serotonin, a neurotransmitter that helps modulate numerous body functions, such as mood, metabolism, sexuality and sleep. Vitamin B6, found in bananas, potatoes, prunes and chickpeas, can relieve irritability and stress. B6 does this by raising your levels of dopamine. Dopamine is the "feel-good" neurotransmitter.

"**Sweet potatoes** contain beta-carotene, Vitamin C and Vitamin E. Those nutrients play a role in preventing heart disease and cancer. Sweet potatoes contain lots of fiber that makes them an excellent choice for people with diabetes. The folate and B6 they contain also provide a brain boost." *

"**Tangerines** stop free radicals with Vitamin C, Vitamin A and beta-cryptoxanthin. Most importantly, tangerines contain tangeretin and nobiletin, which are extremely potent against certain types of breast cancer." *

"**Tea** is truly 'a cup of good health.' Want to buy a beverage that stops cancer of the skin, lung, stomach, colon, liver, breast, esophagus, pancreas and the small intestine, while reducing the risk of heart disease and stroke? It's tea!

"Black tea, Darjeeling and Earl Grey lower the risk of heart disease and colon cancer and prevent dental cavities. Green tea, such as Jewel Green or Japanese Sencha, prevents many kinds of cancer and boosts immunity. Oolong tea is a cross between green and black it helps with itchy skin rashes.

"White tea is the least processed and contains more anti-oxidants than the others. An animal study demonstrated that it prevents precancerous colon tumors." *

"**Tomatoes** contain lycopene, a potent antioxidant. People who ate seven or more servings a week had a 60% lower chance of developing stomach, colon and rectal cancers than people who ate two servings or less.

"Lycopene concentrates in the prostate; thus ten servings a week lowers the risk for prostate cancer. Tomatoes also contain coumaric acid and chlorogenic acid, which may help block nitrosamines that form naturally in the body. Nitrosamines are the most potent carcinogen in tobacco smoke! Smokers, eat your tomatoes! Tomatoes contain Vitamin C, Vitamin A and iron; all three are important nutrients for health." *

Tropical fruits aid in digestion to prevent heart disease and cancer. (See guavas, mango, papaya, and pomegranate.)

Walnuts contain ellagic acid, an antioxidant that helps battle cancer.

Water in sufficient quantities is essential for good health. In the wonderful book, *The Doctor's Book of Food Remedies,* I learned about the virtues of water. I was astonished to learn that not drinking enough water can be as harmful to your heart as smoking. "Not having enough water can cause fatigue, a symptom leading to many doctor's visits. Did you know that water can wash away weight? Drinking water is a good way to calm hunger pains. Also, when you drink cold water you actually burn more calories as the body warms the water to 98.6 degrees.

"The way to tell if you are getting enough water is by the color of your urine. The color of urine should be pale and clear. If it is dark, you should drink more water. Other fluids such as coffee, soda and milk do not replace clear, clean water." *

Watercress is a member of the cruciferous vegetable family. Cruciferous should be synonymous with cancerfighting vegetable family. I would have thought watercress was for small cream cheese sandwiches at high tea. In other words, not to be taken too seriously. Was I wrong!

Watercress is particularly potent against lung cancer because it contains PEITC. PEITC are trigger enzymes that disarm carcinogens. It also contains antioxidants, betacarotene, Vitamin C and Vitamin E, which scavenge free radicals from our bodies. In this way, watercress may help with wrinkles and protect the eyes too! Don't put watercress directly on the eyes as you may have seen with cucumbers. Just remember to eat watercress in your little cream cheese sandwiches.

Wine is controversial. As you may remember, alcohol is a very potent risk in breast cancer. But red wine is the secret to a healthy heart. What to do??

First, assess your genetic risks for breast cancer, then your family history for heart health. If most of your relatives died early from heart-related issues, you may want to have some red wine every day. The secret is not to have more than one glass!

A supplement called Trans-Resveratrol can be taken without the risk of alcohol consumption but with all the benefits of drinking red wine. The benefits include keeping blood platelets from sticking together and forming clots.

"Studies suggest that bacteria and traveler's diarrhea can be stopped by red and white wine. Also, red wine contains saponins and flavonoids, which may cool body inflammation, thereby reducing the risk of heart disease and cancer. The richest source of saponins and flavonoids is to be found in red Zinfandel, followed by Syrah, Pinot Noir and Cabernet Sauvignon. Of interest is the fact that with one or two glasses a day, people were 54% less likely to be obese than nondrinkers. " * Four or more glasses a day have proven to be antiproductive, not only for cancer but also for obesity. People who drank four or more glasses a day were 50% more likely to be obese than nondrinkers. So now we have the skinny on wine drinking!

Wound healing is of particular interest to me after having five surgeries in as many months. I can assure you wound healing was also a very important matter to Dr. Orringer, my reconstructive plastic surgeon. Adequate protein consumption is advised for optimal healing. It is not the time to cut back on eating to lose those few extra pounds. Dr. Orringer often reminded me to eat protein four times a day. I had to be reminded because when taking antibiotics, my appetite goes way down. I felt nauseous and not motivated to eat. Therefore, make sure you eat plenty of fish, steak, beans, nuts and grains while healing. The other two important components to healing are Vitamin C and zinc. Tissue strength relies on Vitamin C. And zinc helps tissues grow and repair. Oysters are an excellent source of zinc. I ate them often following my surgeries.

"For a final boost to your healing, add Omega-3s, walnuts and flaxseed. Finally, eat your organic carrots or juice. The Vitamin A will help collagen formation and skin reproduction." *

Yogurt and probiotics are everywhere we look nowadays. Probiotics put back into our intestines what nature intended to be there. "Healing cultures that treat yeast infections, ease lactose intolerance and boost our immunity."*

BENEFITS OF HEALTHY DIETS

The Mediterranean Diet reduces the risk of heart disease and cancer. This diet contains lots of fruits and vegetables, whole grains and nuts. Lamb and chicken are consumed infrequently. The main source of fat is from olive oil. They eat fish for Omega-3s and they get lots of exercise. They drink red wine frequently, usually with every meal.

A vegetarian diet is often perceived as the road to a long life, according to my gynecologist, Dr. Uzzi Reiss, and many other doctors. After my bout with breast cancer, Dr. Reiss urged me to eat mostly vegetables.

"Do this and you will end up burying your husband," he told me.

I don't think that made me feel any better, but the point was made! A vegetable-based diet, low in saturated fat and high in fiber, antioxidants and vitamins will put you on the road to a healthier and longer life. Research on vegetarians showed they have lower rates of cancer, heart disease and high blood pressure.

Meanwhile, a low-fat diet helps keep the body bodacious and reduces the risk of heart disease, prevents cancer, promotes weight loss and preserves good vision. "In a Nigerian study, researchers found rats fed high-fat diets began producing enzymes that lead to cancerous change in the colon in three weeks." *

By paying attention to what you eat and making choices based on the health benefits, you can win in the battle against cancer. I have given you much information about these foods and your health with a major thrust on cancer prevention. Therefore, I would urge you to read *The Doctor's Book of Food Remedies* by Selene Yeager and the editors of Prevention, Rodole Inc. You will find more foods listed for various reasons other than cancer prevention.

Six

Herbs That Heal

*H*erbs have been used for centuries as remedies for ailments and to maintain health, long before prescription drugs existed as the magic cure-all for every illness and symptom. Now, a substantial body of knowledge exists about herbs and their uses to protect the body. This chapter draws from that information to present just a brief overview of what I learned about some of the ways I could protect my own health.

I've organized the information into three sections: specific ailments and the herbs to restore health, ways to boost the immune system, and substances that combat flu and colds and aid respiration, since drawing in life-giving oxygen is essential to health!

To preface this chapter, I would be remiss if I didn't acknowledge the exceptional book, Herbs for Health and Healing by Kathi Keville. Ms. Keville is the Director of the American Herb Association. She has provided a plethora of useful information to assist us in our quest for a more healthy lifestyle. In the following section,"Herbs That Heal," I have used excerpts from her book that I felt would give readers a good jump-start on their way to learning herbal remedies. I highly recommend reading Ms. Keville's book in its entirety. You will be amazed at its depth and healthier for your efforts.

When you see quote marks with an asterisk (" *) at the end of a sentence you may assume the words are from Kathi Keville. So, let's begin!

RESTORING HEALTH

Below is a list of some common ailments and the life-giving herbs to combat them that are readily available nowadays, not in just health food stores but even big supermarkets and chain stores. That's because the recognition of their benefits is becoming more and more accepted.

Alcohol is enjoyable—a few glasses of wine or a few beers with friends just seems sociable—but we all know that cutting way down on drinking is suggested for cancer prevention. You will find a friend in evening primrose oil and valerian for this purpose.

Anemia can be treated with parsley, watercress and seaweed dulse. Avoid black tea because it blocks iron absorption.

Anxiety leads to severe stress on the body and stress is our enemy. Therefore, kava and valerian have been shown to help with this disorder.

Arthritis "responds well to licorice, ginseng, CLA and echinacea." *

Constipation "is not good from any standpoint but the one downside we are most concerned with is carcinogens. When we ingest food or drink we digest them. What are left are waste products. We know some of them are harmful byproducts such as pesticides! When we eat enough fiber and drink lots of water we pass the by-products along faster. Therefore, they have less time to react with our bodies and intestinal tract." *

"Stay away from pastries, refined flour and white rice if you experience constipation often. Take psyllium, eat prunes and massage the abdomen with essential oils such as chamomile and peppermint to keep things moving." *

Depression is so widespread that antidepressants are a big business and for good reason. Many people report feelings of despair and apathy. It's important to know that depression is the opposite of expression.

Depression is the opposite of expression! When we express our emotions instead of depressing them we feel better. A wonderful circle of friends can help tremendously with your mental health. A trio of herbs is also useful; they are ginseng, licorice and St. John's wort.

Headache herbal remedies include ginger tea or the herb, feverfew. When I used to get a lot of migraines I tried feverfew. At that time I did not respond to it, but I didn't know about the anti-inflammatory effects of ginger. I find ginger to be some kind of wonderful herb.

Insomnia can zap our zest for life. Without a good night's sleep most anything is a chore. We drag ourselves around uninspired. Therefore, it is prudent to try different remedies to help us get a good night's sleep. "St. John's wort, chamomile and valerian taken a few times in the day with a larger dose before bed may be the answer. In Europe, the most popular sleeping aid is passionflower." * So let's get some passion in our lives!

Memory "can be improved using ginkgo, ginseng and gotu kola since they are associated with improving brain function. There is a Chinese herb called club moss that is being given to patients with Alzheimer's disease." * After working with Alzheimer's patients and their families in my psychotherapy practice, I'm for exhausting all possibilities in order to help these individuals and their families as they struggle with this difficult disease! At this time, Aricept® is a drug developed to help the brain synapses communicate with each other. I am not opposed to a better life through chemistry, but natural products sometimes work just as well as their drug counterparts. Also, sometimes both may be given, but always under a doctor's care to intensify the effect of each one. A doctor must be consulted because combining drugs and herbs must be done carefully to be sure they mix well together.

Pain is caused by inflammation and swelling. "Pain leads to long-term stress and possibly depression." * Herbs that help with inflammation can help reduce pain. And that's a good thing. Willow bark from where we get aspirin contains salicin, which works by reducing the production of prostaglandins. Bromelain from the pineapple works by the production of prostaglandins also. Eat your pineapple when you feel inflammation in your joints. "CLA from evening primrose oil and echinacea are anti-inflammatory as well." *

"Turmeric (curcumin) has been shown to be as effective as cortisone and phenylbutazone in decreasing inflammation." * Suggested herbs for nerve and muscle pain are St. John's wort, chamomile with valerian, hops and passionflower.

Recently at an herb store I was visiting, one gentleman described inflammation as inflam-aging! In other words, we do not want inflammation in our bodies or we will age prematurely.

A topical cream for pain I have used with great success is capsaicin cream. It is made from cayenne and short circuits the pain response. Be sure not to rub your eyes after applying capsaicin cream; it's not a very pleasant experience, I can vouch for that!

Stress seems so prevalent; what can help? The B vitamins are called the stress vitamins. If you're like me, B vitamins in any effective dose may upset your stomach. Therefore, I take mine individually and at different times of the day. Valerian, chamomile and passionflower are calming and sedative herbs. "Stress takes a great toll on our adrenal glands that can and often does lead to adrenal exhaustion. Licorice, ligustrum with Siberian ginseng are often prescribed for this problem." * "In Polynesia, kava tea is used to induce relaxation, restful sleep and mild euphoria." * The Polynesians say kava promotes peace and harmony among people. We could all use a little of that!

THE IMMUNE SYSTEM

Immune-related diseases are on the rise such as asthma, cancer, chronic fatigue syndrome, Epstein-Barr, multiple sclerosis and psoriasis. "When we are experiencing allergies or an asthmatic episode, our immune system is responding over aggressively to a harmless substance such as pollen or dust. The autoimmune disorder falsely identifies harmless substances as dangerous invaders then sets out to attack and kill them, in the process injuring body tissue. Some examples are lupus, rheumatoid arthritis, pernicious anemia and Addison's disease, which are defined as partial or complete adrenal failure." * T cells are a group of white blood cells that protect our body's immunity and includes special, Natural Killer T cells that destroy threats to our body. "Our natural immunity or T cells are lowered by emotional or physical stress, poor diet, smoking and too much alcohol." * Even positive stress such as a vacation, wedding or a new home can suppress our T cells and let cancer cells survive. The herbs and foods listed below help boost the immune system.

Artichokes "are part of the thistle family; they protect the liver but be sure to get organic because conventional artichokes are heavily sprayed with pesticides. Antioxidants in the milk thistle called fla-vonoids are the most potent liverprotecting substances known." *

Burdock has been shown to inhibit and slow growth from can-cerous tumors.

Dandelion, chamomile, licorice and especially milk thistle can help a damaged liver because a damaged liver will make you feel like hell and eventually kill you.

Here's a restorative "liver tea…dandelion root, milk thistle seeds, licorice root and ginger root. Let steep 15 minutes in 1 quart of water. Drink at least 1 cup a day." *

Echinacea is the apex of immunity herbs. Echinacea increases the T cells but also increases interferon and Natural Killer cells, special types of white blood cells that include Natural Killer T cells. It works best if taken as needed not on a continuous basis. "Take echinacea when you have an active infection. The root and seeds have the strongest immune properties. They can be hard to find, but if possible, they are most effective. Echinacea tea or liquid must taste bitter otherwise it's not strong enough or doesn't contain echinacea at all." * In Chinese medicine, echinacea is often used with ligustrum to enhance results.

Garlic and onion help with stomach cancer.

"**Siberian ginseng** decreased toxic effects of chemotherapy used to treat breast cancer." *

"**Gotu kola, kelp and dandelion** inhibit tumors." *

Licorice is another great immunity enhancer that works well with the herpes virus. "Licorice has been found to neutralize liver toxins. Licorice also increased the production of interferon, which is commonly used to treat hepatitis B." *

Milk thistle can help with "repairing the liver from heavy metal poisoning. And don't think that you have to work in a factory to get heavy metal poisoning. Heavy metals are all around us, lead in tin cans, mercury in dental fillings and cosmetics, aluminum in antacids." *

"**Paudarco tea** reduced pain in cancer patients. Herbalists use it to treat immune related disorders such as asthma, eczema, psoriasis, shingles and yeast infections." *

Red clover has some of the same effects as burdock.

The "**shitake mushroom** is more effective than medicinal antivirals, such as Flumedine, for fighting viruses."*

"The herb **Shizandra** has been proven to diminish hepatitis B in less than a month. Chronic hepatitis needs reishi mushrooms, shizandra and astragulus. Add ginger to the mix to enhance the efficiency of the formula. Ginger helps the other herbs work better." *

Thyme in small amounts can reduce your risk of cancer. Basil and turmeric do the same.

COMBATING FLU AND COLDS:

HELPING THE RESPIRATORY TRACT

When you feel the first sign of cold or flu, take a day or two in bed with a bowl of chicken soup. This is not a luxury but a necessity! Unless the body gets some rest it cannot properly fight the infection. Think twice about lowering a fever. I know it feels better to lower the fever but fever is the body's natural defense against invaders. Let the fever be, if it's around 101 or 102 degrees; anything over may require lowering.

A **cough** can be beneficial to clear airways, therefore, do not always prevent a cough; usually prevention at night to sleep is best.

"**Asthma** is an allergic reaction; **pneumonia** can be viral or bacterial in nature. **Bronchitis** is an infection of the bronchi." * Even when the infection is cleared, a bronchial cough can persist for weeks or even months making this condition extremely disconcerting.

Meanwhile, below are some other remedies that can help.

"**Cayenne** gargle can be made using 1/8 teaspoon cayenne powder, 1/4 cup of water, stir and gargle." *

Elderberry syrup is antiviral syrup developed by a virologist. Elderberry syrup may even inhibit herpes and Epstein-Barr virus; it tastes good too. I try to keep a bottle of it in my kitchen at all times.

"**Essential oil steam** helps combat the flu and laryngitis. Take 3 cups of water, 1/4 teaspoon eucalyptus or peppermint oil. Bring water to simmer, turn off heat. Place face over the pot and drape a towel over your head, then breathe in the steam." * Come out for fresh air as needed and get great looking skin in the process!

Garlic is nature's antibiotic. "Plantains (the fried bananas in some ethnic dishes) are helpful for coughing, wheezing and chest pain from bronchitis. Berberine, goldenseal and Oregon grape root have antibiotic properties. Some antiallergy natural antihista-mines are chamomile, peppermint, ginger, anise and feverfew." *

Siberian **ginseng**, echinacea, shizandra and astragalus help build natural resistance and are natural flu fighters.

Licorice works a lot like echinacea.

"Herbal expectorants are **mullein**, thyme, horehound and elecampane. One of nature's best lung herbs, elecampane, was routinely given to people with asthma in England. They would chew a piece in the morning and the evening." *

Onion is one old-fashioned herbal remedy to take seriously! I know onions and garlic do not make for sweet breath, but they do many miraculous things for your body.

They are antibiotic and anti-inflammatory. Make an "onion syrup using…1 onion, 2 cups of water, 3 tablespoons of honey. Gently simmer onion in water for 20 minutes, then blend it with the water and finally add the honey. Take a tablespoon at a time as warm as possible." *

"**Yarrow**, elderflowers and peppermint help with chronic sinus congestion…they help to reduce inflamed sinuses and help them drain." * Don't forget to use Dr. Weil's Neti Pot or bulb syringe with saline solution for nasal irrigation.

Simple saltwater can be an effective respiratory aid, according to Dr. Weil.

"Flushing your nose with saltwater is one of the most effective techniques I know to clear out mucus, allergens and other irritants. Some research has found it helpful for treating chronic sinusitis as well as hay fever and other seasonal allergies. I also believe it can benefit people with colds, postnasal drip, dryness in the nose and other sinus problems."

Source: Dr. Andrew Weil from his Essential Guide to Natural Healing.

So now we have an idea about foods for health and herbs that heal. The reason I say an idea is because these subjects are vast. Foods and herbs could easily take up volumes on their own. I have presented a primer course in order to start you on your way to health. Please understand that the information presented was derived from two books I researched for my own personal quest. I am not a medical doctor, therefore, understand the opinions given are not mine; they are imparted to you from the text. I encourage you to explore these subjects further and always check with your doctor before including these herbs and procedures in your routine.

Seven

GOOD PRACTICES FOR WOMEN'S HEALTH

*E*ating well and taking herbal remedies are just part of the journey to good health. We, as women, also have specific and special health needs. We need to follow good medical practices that help us stay in the best health we possibly can. For that reason, I am providing ways that women can keep themselves healthy by following good medical practices.

I also address menopause; the wondrous drug, aspirin, and dental health, often a neglected part of our health.

BREAST SELF-EXAMS

Almost all women I spoke to, including my best friends, do not do routine breast self-exams. This saddens and concerns me since I found my breast cancer in the shower. Many women feel that self-exam is almost equivalent to masturbation. Something to shy away from and certainly not talk about. I can assure you ladies you will not go blind or be struck down by lightning for giving your breasts a good feel. As a matter of fact, I saved my own life this way and you can too.

I urge and encourage all of you to become intimately familiar with your own breasts. By this I mean a breast exam should not be hurried or taken lightly.

Some form of lubricant is always better for detecting abnormalities. In my case, it was the shower gel. I would like to suggest that once a month, preferably at the same time of the month, you perform your breast self-exam. Choose a time when you will not be disturbed. Step into the shower or bath, let the warm water relax you so you do not rush the procedure.

Feel both the left and right side of the chest. Note any cystic abnormalities. A lot of us have cystic breasts due to hormone changes and too many Starbucks! Make a chart of the left and right breasts, jot down anything you feel or see under the skin that concerns you. Go over this with your doctor. Even when your concerns have been ruled out as anything serious, you should always check your breasts for the same irregularities. You will be looking for anything that is different or was not there the month before! Check your chart to be sure. Be sure to feel all the way to the collarbone, under the arms and entire chest wall down the bottom of the ribs. Now pat yourself on the back for doing such a good job.

ESTROGEN

Estrogen makes us feel good. We have energy for life, we take on new adventures and explore new possibilities. We feel sensual and feminine, our skin has fewer wrinkles and remains moist. Too much estrogen, on the other hand, makes us have the jitters and become overly sensitive. It can lead to endometriosis, fibroids, uterine cancer, breast cysts and breast cancer.

I had breast cysts and fibroids for several years; maybe I should have lowered my estrogen intake from E1 to E3, the milder form of estrogen years ago. They say everything is 20/20 in hindsight and I believe that's true. I would caution others that have similar symptoms to cut back if they are taking HRT, but always check with your doctor first.

CERVICAL DYSPLASIA

Cervical Dysplasia is caused by the HPV or genital wart virus also called the herpes virus. A folic acid deficiency can also contribute to this condition. "A little-known fact is that smoking even 2 or 3 cigarettes a day seems to concentrate carcinogen in the cervix." *

"Calendula is an herb with an affinity for healing the cervix." * Also suggested by the writer, Kathi Keville, is a way to put herbs directly on the cervix, by using echinacea tea and calendula-soaked tampons.

FIBROCYSTIC BREASTS

Too much estrogen, stress, fat and alcohol intake are the culprits. Also, methylxanthines such as coffee, cola, tea and chocolate! I love coffee, tea, cola and chocolate! That is why I thought the breast lump I felt was the result of too much coffee. I'm glad I followed up as soon as I did, even though there was a logical explanation for the lump. So don't rationalize lumps in your breast; it's better to be safe than sorry. Check things out as soon as possible.

MAMMOGRAMS REVISITED

I know mammograms do find breast cancer, but as I mentioned earlier, not always. So please do not discontinue your yearly mammograms without consulting your doctor. And do not let yourself have a false sense of security. It is a must to perform breast self-exams regularly. Also, I don't believe in the antiquated machines that still are used so often. There are technologically advanced mammography systems that provide less radiation to the breast and images that are superior. So be sure your mammograms are digital and don't let the tech squeeze until you scream. Always have your test results reviewed by a breast radiologist. A breast radiologist is a physician with a totally devoted practice to the subspecialty field of breast imaging, highly regarded in the analysis of breast films.

Add adjunct screening if there is any doubt in your mind about a breast lump; they include breast ultrasound and breast

MRI. Be vigilant because studies have shown time and time again that survival rates in women diagnosed with breast cancer is dependent on how early it is found.

PERIODS

A remedy for "**heavy periods**: 1 teaspoon tincture Shepard's purse and yarrow leaf. Red raspberry also reduces bleeding and strengthens the uterus." *

PROGESTERONE

"It reduces stress, water retention and muscle weakness, and helps the body handle alcohol, sugar and food cravings. Too much can make you feel sluggish, lower blood sugar, increase appetite and weight gain." *

Johns Hopkins gave a group of women 800 units of Vitamin E for 10 weeks. They found Vitamin E corrects the estrogen/

progesterone ratio, increases libido and normalizes menstrual cycles.

"We all know that a healthy liver is important, but most of us don't know the liver deactivates estrogen especially the carcinogenic form that settles in the breast and uterus." * "Liver herbs such as burdock and dandelion, also milk thistle help us with difficult to treat health problems." *

WATER RETENTION

Avoid salt and take natural diuretics like asparagus and dandelion.

VAGINAL INFECTIONS

Vaginal infections are often caused by antibiotic use. So what can be done when your doctor prescribes antibiotics for you? "Herbal remedies are effective in treating many infections such as yeast and chlamydia. Vaginal douche containing lavender, tea tree and yogurt kill harmful microorganisms including yeast and trichomonas." * Eating yogurt as soon as you start antibiotics can also help.

Menopause

Menopause begins in most women around age 50. It is defined as not having a period for one year. With the ending of periods and sharp decline of hormones, havoc comes to home to roost.

Common symptoms include anxiety, weepiness, fatigue, weight gain, hot flashes, depression, confusion, sleeplessness, loss of muscle tone, skin and vaginal dryness to name a few. Some herbs have been suggested to help with these symptoms. Black cohosh with Vitamin E for hot flashes, ginseng for stamina, red clover, flaxseed and soy. Soy contains natural phytoestrogens. Mexican wild yam provides natural progesterone. "Pomegranate seeds, rhubarb, pineapple,nuts and avocados contain some estro- gen- like compounds." *

Suzanne Somers on Menopause

"Then suddenly, the Seven Dwarfs of menopause arrived at my door without warning: Itchy, Bitchy, Sweaty, Sleepy, Bloated, Forgetful and All Dried Up. One by one they crept into my private cottage in the woods and started to take over my life. For me, the first to arrive was Itchy. I developed this itch on my right calf that was so irritating, I wanted to scratch the skin right off my body. Then Bitchy came to my door. No longer was my PMS contained to one or two days a month, it felt like constant PMS. Then I would swing from Bitchy to Weepy, for God's sake, what was wrong with me? Ding–dong…it's the middle of the night and Sweaty has crawled into bed with me. Oh yes, Sweaty brought embarrassing hot flashes and intro- duced me to night sweats where it seemed as if a faucet had been attached between my breasts. Of course, Sweaty brought along Sleepy because I was tired all the time. I would wake up so many times in the night and not be able to get back to sleep.

Bloated crept in slowly. My once svelte figure got thick through the middle section, even though I was following my weight loss program that had worked so well for so many years! I can't quite remember when Forgetful arrived, but one day my brain stopped working. Lastly, All Dried Up slowly encroached upon my happy marriage. This was probably the most unpleasant of all the dwarf family. Sex was no longer on the top of my list… or on my list at all. My husband would give me that knowing look, and I would think, "Frankly, I'd rather have a smoothie."

As you probably can see from Suzanne's comments about the Seven Dwarfs of Menopause, she did not have an easy transition in her life at that time. But God bless her! She wrote books to help all of us through our own misery. I highly recommend you read at least one of Suzanne's books if you are experiencing difficulties with menopause.

Remember, you are not alone, many women are feeling exactly the same way, they just don't talk about it. So, become informed.

Try herbs to see if they can help you. Some women make enough estrogen from adipose tissue to get by with herbs alone. Many of us will need hormone replacement. Whatever the solution is, be stubborn, don't give in to the comment, "You're getting older, what do you expect?" Stick with your quest for optimal health. Although the road may be bumpy and take you for some curves, you will eventually get there with some tenacity and good humor.

Aspirin

During my research I encountered much information about aspirin. With all the new painkillers on the market, this older, even old-fashioned drug, was overlooked. But in reading a July issue of *Life Extension* magazine, I encountered some eye-opening information.

Source: Life Extension, July 2006.

Remarkable research uncovers lifesaving benefits beyond cardiovascular protection. Ask any doctor what drug they would want with them if stranded on a desert island, and most would say aspirin…why is that?

Aspirin for many years has been known as a miracle drug. It reduces blood clotting, fever, inflammation and pain. Recently it has been added to many men's health programs for cardiovascular health. My husband has been taking 81 mg (equivalent to a baby aspirin) every day for about five years now.

Life Extension magazine has long warned that chronic inflammation can pave the way for many deadly diseases, including cancer. Inflammation plays many roles in encouraging normal cells to become cancerous. The inflammatory process in the body is our enemy; therefore, aspirin reduces inflammation and the resulting cancer.

ASPIRIN REDUCES BREAST CANCER

A study in 2005 noted that women who used more than 100 mg of aspirin on a frequent basis prior to mammogram testing had a lower risk of breast cancer than infrequent users or nonusers of aspirin.

ASPIRIN AND SKIN CANCER

People who had used aspirin or other NSAIDs at least twice a week for five years reduced their risk of skin cancer by 60%; those who used aspirin daily for five years saw an amazing decrease of nearly 90% in the risk of developing skin cancer!

ASPIRIN AND COLON CANCER

One study in 2003 examined 635 patients with a history of colorectal cancer. Half took 325 mg of aspirin a day; the other half took a placebo. After a year each group underwent a colonoscopy to check for polyps. The subjects in the aspirin group had a 35% lower risk of polyps than the placebo group. Also, it took longer for polyps to develop in the subjects who took aspirin.

ASPIRIN AND ALZHEIMER'S DISEASE

Regular use of anti-inflammatory drugs, particularly aspirin, has been associated with lower incidence of Alzheimer's disease. If taken for 24 months the results are amazing: 73% reduced risk of developing the disease. Furthermore, this group maintained better cognitive function than those who did not use aspirin.

After reviewing all this information I decided to consider taking aspirin. I have been avoiding aspirin because of a sensitive stomach. The answer may be in a baby dose of enteric aspirin (one that dissolves after it leaves the stomach). With all this said, it might be worth considering aspirin as a staple in your medicine cabinet! Caution: Individuals with allergies to aspirin or other salicylates should not use aspirin. People with a history of bleeding disorders, hemorrhagic stroke, asthma or ulcers should speak with a doctor before using aspirin. Consult a physician before using aspirin in combination with over-the-counter or prescription medication. Children and teenagers with symptoms of flu or chicken pox should not take aspirin.

DENTAL HEALTH

According to Prevention Healthy Woman (2005), a costly health mistake is forgetting to floss your teeth. Today just look around you and you will probably notice a lot of very white teeth. Americans spend $600 million a year on procedures to bleach their teeth. But they do not take the five minutes a day it takes to floss. The result: 23% of women between 30 and 54, and 44% of women over 55, have severe gum disease.

Gum disease is a serious bacterial infection; it's the number one cause of tooth loss. Putting the cosmetic issues aside, periodontal disease can cause havoc with your health. When periodontal bacteria enter the bloodstream, they can travel to major organs and cause chronic inflammation. Researchers have speculated recently that such simmering infections may cause some cases of heart disease, stroke, cancer and premature birth.

So be sure to floss at least once a day and take good care of your pearly whites because dental health affects more than your teeth and gums.

Eight

Aromatherapy, Yoga & Massage

Keeping calm, positive and focused is essential to staying well. You can eat all the right foods, ingest all the right herbs, follow the best medical practices, but if your life is hectic and out of balance and you take no time to calm yourself, all your healthy living efforts can be undone.

That's why I've written this chapter about aromatherapy, yoga and massage. These can help bring about the peace you need to move forward in health.

Aromatherapy

"Whether the scent of coconut transports you back to your tropical vacation or the aroma of freshly baked cookies reminds you of your grandmother's kitchen, it's clear that smell has a powerful influence on the mind."
—*Dr. Andrew Weil.*

Certain smells have profound effects on how we feel: For example, the scent of lavender is used for calming and restful sleep. Use citrus fragrance when you need an energy boost. The scent of rosemary has been used for grief and sorrow. Eucalyptus steam clears congestion and appears to reduce mucus production. The oil of grapefruit stimulates production of natural painkillers called enkephalins. A whiff of green apple has been said to reduce hunger.

Alertness can be increased with use of rosemary, according to Dr. Weil, who says that, " the culinary herb rosemary has a reputation as a memory aid, and research supports this idea".

Source: Dr. Andrew Weil, International Journal of Neuroscience, *January 2003).*

Anxiety, can be decreased using the fragrance of oranges or lavender. According to the results of a study published in *Physiology and Behavior* magazine, of 200 dental patients those exposed to either the smell of orange or lavender before dental work had less anxiety than persons exposed to no odors.

Source: Physiology and Behavior, *September 15, 2005.*

Meanwhile, for headache relief, research in Germany suggests that peppermint oil rubbed on the temples and forehead can reduce the intensity of a tension headache.

For libido, recent research to determine which scents boosted sexual arousal found that women responded to licorice, cucumber and baby powder. For men, pumpkin pie won.

Meanwhile, research on sleep found that among 31 young adults those exposed to the scent of lavender slept more deeply and felt more refreshed in the morning.

Chronobiology International, *September 2005.*

According to Dr. Weil, "In France, aromatherapy has long been accepted as a form of medicinal practice. Research is now validating aromatherapy as a medical modality for many conditions. If you decide to consult an aromatherapist, make sure his or her training matches your expectations. If you simply want to relieve stress, a massage therapist or even a beautician with aromatherapy training may suit you. But for help with a physical complaint, find someone with greater depth of training."

Source: Dr. Andrew Weil, Essential Guide to Natural Healing, Fall 2007.

If you'd like more information, another resource is the book, *Essential Aromatherapy* by Susan Worwood and Valerie Ann Worwood (New World Library, 2003).

YOGA

We know stress is our enemy. Being overweight damages our joints and can contribute to breast cancer. Moving our bodies is important not only for physical health but has been proven to reduce stress and improve our moods. Walking and swimming have been touted as the best exercises for healthful results with minimum wear on the body. Now, you can add another physical therapy to your arsenal and that is yoga.

According to Dr. Weil, "more than 16 million Americans practice yoga regularly…while some see yoga as a gentle form of exercise, others use it as a relaxation technique or as valuable therapy for conditions ranging from asthma to back pain to hypertension. Still others consider it a path to spiritual fulfillment. Truth is, yoga is all of these things, and it's suitable for individuals of all ages".

A review of nine studies involving cancer patients and survivors found yoga yielded improvements in sleep quality, mood, stress, and overall *quality of life*.

Source: Cancer Control, July 2005.

Yoga's increasing popularity may be due to its mainstreaming into the medical community. For example, Dr. Dean Ornish founder and president of the nonprofit Preventive Medicine Research Institute in Sausalito, Calif., includes yoga in his lifestyle program which is proving to reduce heart disease. Many medical models for addiction intervention and anxiety disorder therapies incorporate meditation and yoga.

Although yoga is a gentle form of exercise, always make sure you listen to your own body. Never, never do any pose that causes pain. Consult your doctor for any suggestions he or she may have concerning your exercise program.

And always, get referrals for qualified teachers in your area. Namaste. ("The light within me honors the light within you.")

Massage Therapy

The purpose of the practice of massage therapy is to enhance general health and a feeling of well-being to the client. Massage therapy has been around in one form or another since ancient times. One way to know if something has value is too see if it's a fad and hence ceases to exist or lasts the tests of time. Massage therapy has proven its value in this way.

A massage therapist will use structured palpitation or movement of the soft tissues out of the body. In this way, the therapist relieves congestion and releases muscle spasm providing relaxation and pain relief.

A little known fact about massage therapy is that it meets our unmet dependency needs. In other words, if a person has not had a warm mother or father or did not receive ample hugging and acceptance in their childhood, they have unmet dependency needs. Massage can help heal the hole in the soul!

Some things massage does not include are: diagnosis of pathology, recommendations for drugs or spinal manipulations or anything else that lies outside the scope of massage therapy.

That being said, there are many benefits and different forms of massage. Too many actually to mention in this book. I have included the most well known forms of massage and they are as follows:

SWEDISH MASSAGE

One of the most well known and commonly taught massage techniques. Swedish massage is a treatment designed to energize and relax the body by increasing circulation. This is the massage most often offered at hotel spas. You will be asked to disrobe, but you will be covered by a sheet. The therapist will use oil to reduce friction on the skin. Aromatic oils may be used at the same time to enhance the relaxation process. The therapist uses a combination of kneading, rolling and tapping movements to speed healing and reduce swelling in certain parts of the body. Usually more gentle than deep tissue or sports massage, even clients that are sensitive to the touch can enjoy this type of massage.

For those of you that choose not to disrobe in public and feel a little icky about that, all is not lost. The benefits of massage can be so profound on your mental and physical health; I am mentioning the chair massage as an alternative.

Chair Massage

Known as the seated massage or on-site massage, it involves the use of a specially designed massage chair in which the client sits comfortably. The modern chair massage was developed by David Palmer, but seated massage is a centuries old Japanese technique. Chair massage is provided to the fully clothed client in a variety of settings, including airports, businesses, and even shopping malls. So ladies, no excuses to avoid this very healthful form of therapy.

Deep Tissue Massage

Deep tissue has in a certain way saved my life. I practically crawl into my sessions sometimes. Fibromyalgia can set my muscles up for great pain and spasms. Deep tissue is not always the most relaxing experience but definitely the most physically gratify-ing when over. Deep tissue techniques affect the sub layer of musculature and fascia. The techniques require advanced train-ing. Muscles must first be relaxed in order to effectively perform deep tissue massage. Heat applied for 20 minutes prior to the massage will allow the therapist to reach into deep tissue mus-culature. Deep tissue helps with muscle pain and injury reha-bilitation. Also effective in reducing pain from inflammation of arthritis and tendonitis.

Something I know about deep tissue massage is that it releases me from the muscular 'straight jacket' my body some-times encapsulates me in. I can tell you that the feeling of relief comes very close to good sex.

If your budget doesn't allow for massage but you truly believe you have a medical problem with muscle pain a medical massage may be just the thing for you.

MEDICAL MASSAGE

To perform medical massage requires a background in pathology and utilizes specific treatments to alleviate pain and recover from injury. The therapist usually works from a doctor's prescription as an adjunct therapist within a hospital or physical therapy setting. Therefore, most therapy of this kind is covered by insurance. So, I urge you to check out your insurance policy and hopefully go forward with your therapy.

REFLEXOLOGY

And last but not least is **Reflexology**. I recommend to those of you who have never experienced massage therapy, do not like to disrobe or be touched, those who need to stick a toe into the pond before jumping in, to consider reflexology. Originated in Ancient China, reflexology involves manipulation of specific areas of the foot, hands and ears that corresponds to other parts of the body. Reflexology is used to release congestion of the body's energy called chi, which promotes relaxation and healing, reduction of pain and circulation of blood and lymphatic fluids. It is ideal for stress related illness and emotional disorders. Reflexology is convenient in cases where the body is traumatized by surgery, accident, etc. and direct physical contact is not appropriate.

If you need more information go to www.massagetherapy. com. I love massage and highly recommend it to anyone I love and that's you!

Nine

Stress Relief

*F*inally, besides engaging in disciplines that help you maintain a calm demeanor, actively taking measures to reduce the stress in your life is the best medicine as I explain below. Plus, your own pets and laughter are other ways to cut stress.

REDUCING STRESS

THE DOCTORS, A TELEVISION SHOW ON CBS NETWORK

Recently, on a recommendation of a friend, I began watching "The Doctors" on television. Like other times when I begin writing a book, it seems I was at the right place at the right time. Tuning in one day to the show, Dr. Travis Stork made a remarkable statement I had to jot down. **"Working the night shift causes the risk of breast cancer to rise by 60%"**. I could not believe my ears. Do you think any female employees at hospitals, transatlantic flight attendants and others know they are at risk? Experts estimate that nearly 20% of the working population in developed countries works night shifts.

Take a look at this article I found

Graveyard Shift Linked to Cancer Risk

MSNBC.com, The Associated Press, Thursday, November 29, 2007

"Next month, the International Agency for Research on Cancer, the cancer arm of the World Health Organization, will classify shift work as a probable carcinogen. That will put shift work in the same category as cancer-causing agents like anabolic steroids, ultraviolet radiation and diesel machine exhaust."

MELATONIN THE PRIME SUSPECT

Scientists suspect that shift work is dangerous because it disrupts the circadian rhythm, the body's biological clock. The hormone melatonin, which can suppress tumor development, is normally produced at night. Light shuts down melatonin production, so people working in artificial light at night may have lower melatonin levels, which scientists think can raise their chances of developing cancer.

Also, sleeping in the daytime in a semi dark room will not produce melatonin. The room must be darkened to mimic nighttime. Therefore, anyone whose light and dark schedule was frequently disrupted could theoretically face the same increased cancer risks. So, all you insomniacs, it's time to solve your sleep problems because your sleep disorder may be causing more than an inconvenience.

Mothers all know instinctually that children should go outdoors and get some fresh air. But most of us didn't know that it wasn't necessarily the fresh air as much as it was the "sunshine vitamin". Vitamin D has recently been found to block the development of some cancers, strengthen bones, prevent multiple sclerosis and alleviate winter depression. Mothers deficient in Vitamin D are more likely to have autistic children (new research has uncovered a connection). Dear God!

We certainly understand that sleeping all day and working through the night depletes and individual's Vitamin D levels. No sun, no Vitamin D. "As time has gone by, Vitamin D has raised its head as a sort of ambrosia for cancers", says Dr. Louis Parker, an epidemiologist and a world expert in the environmental exposures that can lead to cancer, or in case of Vitamin D, the lack of exposures that can lead to cancer.

Dr. Parker says 1000 units are well beyond what you can obtain from your diet. Vitamin D is a bit of a rare vitamin; appearing only in fatty fish, cod liver oil and egg yolks. Even if you were to sunbathe in Southern climates, you would not take in 1,000 units. He notes Vitamin D as a factor turning up in study after study. It turns out people with lung and colon cancer are Vitamin D deficient. And it helps the body absorb calcium. In a study examining whether women who took Vitamin D had stronger bones than those who did not take the vitamin. Years later, researchers went back to that study and found that the women who took Vitamin D also had fewer cancers.

If Vitamin D lowers cancer risk, conversely, lack of Vitamin D raises the risk. Therefore, we can see how Dr. Stork's statement makes sense. Night shift workers get no sunlight; therefore, no Vitamin D and cancer risk goes way up.

Also, if you stay out of the sun to prevent skin cancer or slather on copious amounts of sunscreen to prevent premature aging, you will need to add 1,000 units of Vitamin D a day to your diet.

THE HEALING POWER OF ANIMALS

Per "The Tao of Dog" by Belinda Recio:

"As a writer I have the good fortune of being able to work at home, which has many advantages. But the greatest advantage, by far, is that I get to spend a lot of time with my dog.

As anyone who works at a computer all day knows, sitting at a keyboard has its health risks. Prior to sharing my life with a dog, I didn't take the breaks my body and mind needed. But Spooner has a persistent habit of periodically interrupting my work by pushing my hands off the keyboard with his snout. In his way, Spooner reminds me to get out-side and breathe some fresh air, soak up some Vitamin D, stretch my muscles, and actually notice what's happening around me. I might spend a little less time at the computer, but the time I do spend working is more productive because the breaks revitalize me.

Spooner hasn't just changed the way I work; he has also changed the way I walk. When we take our daily walks, Spooner looks at, sniffs, listens to, tastes and touches nearly everything he encounters. Now I take my cues from him and when I walk I try to engage the earthly world with all my senses. Before Spooner, I had become so trapped in my mental abilities of abstraction and analysis that I often forgot to stop and smell the proverbial roses.

This is what dogs----and other animals---do for us: they help us come to our senses—to regain an honest, primal conscious-ness based on experiences, not abstraction.

Excerpts from The Tao of Dog, Organic Spa Magazine, *January / February 2009. Belinda Recio is* Organic Spa Magazine's *editor of nature and psyche. She has published several books on topics ranging from nature to sacred arts.*

Belinda Recio sure was right when she said animals take us out of our heads and bring us back to our senses. Animals for the most part are warm and fuzzy and make great companions. They combat loneliness which itself can cause a lot of mental and physical distress. Animals do not have the defenses humans have developed to deal with our culture. Therefore, they are fonts of unconditional love. The health benefits of exposure to animals range from general well being to increased survival rates after life-threatening diseases. Scientific research has demonstrated that contact with animals lowers blood pressure and cholesterol levels, reduces anxiety and depression, improves sleeping habits, memory and mobility, enhances family life, fosters cognitive development and self-esteem in children.

So, if you can use a little more love in your life, consider a pet. Happy tails and trails to you!!!!

LAUGHTER

And finally, "Laughter Can Help Your Health," according to *The Wellness Newsletter* (Volume 12, Issue 4, Winter 2009).

Studies show that laughter and good humor may boost your immune system by increasing the activity of cells that seek out and destroy abnormal cells such as viruses and tumors.

One study found that heart attack patients who had 30 minutes of humor a day were less likely to have a second heart attack, needed less medicine, and had lower blood pressure.

Laughter may also ease pain, enhance memory, heart and lung function and circulation. Humor can also improve mood, by lifting an emotional depression and help a person cope with stressful living situations. Humor should be positive and upbeat. And remember, if the other person does not laugh, it's not funny. And don't forget to laugh at yourself too.

Before I leave all of you, I would like to list the supplements I take on a daily basis:

-B6, B12, folic acid (general health)

-Magnesium (bone health)

-Estriol (E3) *

-a pinch of testosterone*

-Progesterone capsules*

-DHEA*

-Vitamin D (cancer prevention)

-Melatonin (sleep enhancement and cancer prevention)

-Milk thistle (liver protection)

-Omega-3s for heart health

-Resveratrol (antiaging)

* HRT bioidenticals

Before starting any supplement regime, check with your doctor. Maybe some of the supplements I take might help you too.

Now, as Dr. Laura would say, **"Go do the right thing".** That means take good care of your health not only for yourself but also for your family and friends.

Because *"Your Health is Your Wealth".*

The End

Afterword

I have found my experience with breast cancer a mighty challenge. All along the way I wanted something worthwhile to come out of this experience. I believe the research and resulting book have given me my wish. So many things in our environment contribute to illness. It is my hope that with knowledge, we will all be able to have healthier and happier lives.

Every time I see one of my dear friends burning too many paraffin candles in a confined space, eating albacore tuna almost every night, or having that third cocktail, I get on my soapbox. I do see a change in my friends' behaviors for the better. It is my heartfelt desire that all of you who read *How I Saved My Own*

Life will not only save your own life but you will live a better one.

Fondly,

Ann Hamilton Wallace

Index

Hormones, 37, 43, 51, 52, 53, 59, 70, 71, 111, 124, 165

HRT bioidenticals, 4, 36, 37, 48, 51, 53, 55, 160, 197

Hydrazine, 117

I

Immune System, 44, 89, 112, 116, 125, 139, 146, 147, 195

Immune-related diseases, 146

Indoles, 108

Inflammation

    Cox-2 protein, 57

    Nuclear factor-kappa beta protein, 57, 124

Insomnia, 141

Insulin, 110

Interferon, 148, 150

International Journal of Neuroscience, 176

Iron, 122, 123, 131, 140

Isothiocyanates, 115

Z

www.ingramcontent.com/pod-product-compliance
Lightning Source LLC
LaVergne TN
LVHW051501080426
835509LV00017B/1858